Phonemic Awareness

Beginning-Sound Ideas, Centers, and Reproducibles

- Phonemic Awareness
- Letter Recognition
- Letter-Sound Association

Written and Illustrated by Lucia Kemp Henry

Managing Editor: Allison E. Ward

Editorial Team: Becky S. Andrews, Kimberley Bruck, Karen P. Shelton, Diane Badden, Thad H. McLaurin, Sharon Murphy, Karen A. Brudnak, Sarah Hamblet, Hope Rodgers, Dorothy C. McKinney

Production Team: Lisa K. Pitts, Pam Crane, Rebecca Saunders, Jennifer Tipton Cappoen, Chris Curry, Sarah Foreman, Theresa Lewis Goode, Clint Moore, Greg D. Rieves, Barry Slate, Donna K. Teal, Zane Williard, Tazmen Carlisle, Irene Harvley-Felder, Amy Kirtley-Hill, Kristy Parton, Cathy Edwards Simrell, Lynette Dickerson, Mark Rainey

www.themailbox.com

ISBN10 #1-56234-655-5 • ISBN13 #978-156234-655-3

Manufactured in the United States
10 9 8 7 6 5 4 3 2

Table of Contents

Using Phonemic

Here's what you get for each beginning consonant and beginning vowel sound:

- an adaptable animal alphabet miniposter
- inspiring ideas
- a reproducible headband, necklace, or bracelet to promote parent involvement
- a full-color center that's ready to laminate and use
- a reproducible cut-and-paste picture sort

Use the animal alphabet miniposters (starting on page 7) to create learning aids.

display cards

word wall headers

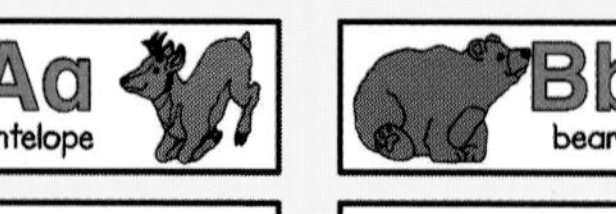

Antoine	Becky	Cade
apple	bat	Conner
	baby	cat

booklet covers

Teach with fun, inspiring ideas.

Choose one or more ideas for teaching or reinforcing the letter sound of your choice.

listen sing pretend dance say move play

Awareness

Sounds Like Fun™

Reinforce with the ready-to-go centers.

Show children how to complete a center. For ease, each center in this book is completed the same way.

Reinforce with reproducibles.

Use the cut-and-paste reproducibles for confidence-building practice.

Show and tell about a sound.

Make headbands, bracelets, or necklaces using the patterns included. Encourage children to wear them home and discuss the sounds with friends and family.

headband

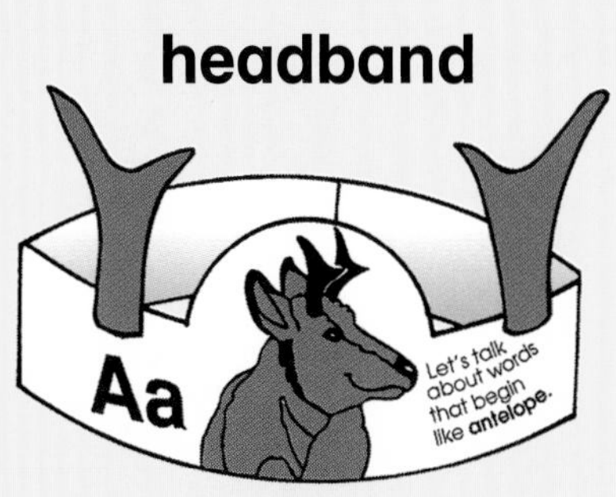

bracelet

necklace

If It's About Sounds, Why the Letters?

Letters are included to give you the *option* of relating the featured sound to its corresponding letter. This option is included because teaching sounds along with alphabet letters helps children begin to see how sounds relate to reading and writing.

The activities, reproducibles, and centers in *Sounds Like Fun: Phonemic Awareness* will work perfectly for your children even if they are not yet ready to focus on letter names, letter forms, or letter-sound relationships.

If you have students who are ready to make observations about letters and begin to associate letters with sounds, you'll find that having the letters on these reproducibles and centers will make that easy too!

Adaptable Animal Alphabet

This section contains a miniposter featuring an animal key word for each letter of the alphabet. Copy them, cut them apart, and use them over and over to promote growth in phonemic awareness, alphabet recognition, and letter-sound association.

Some ways to use the miniposters are

- as display cards **when introducing a sound** and one or more of the corresponding activities in this book
- as labels for a **word wall**
- as **covers for booklets** containing student-made collections of pictures that begin with the indicated sound
- as page labels for a large **student-made alphabet book**
- as a deck of cards for traditional children's **games:** when a child locates (or lands on) a card, he or she names the animal, says its beginning sound, and possibly even names the beginning letter.

apple

baby

antelope

bear

cat

Dd
dog
©The Mailbox® • Sounds Like Fun: Phonemic Awareness • TEC60913
Ee
elephant
©The Mailbox® • Sounds Like Fun: Phonemic Awareness • TEC60913
Ff
fox
©The Mailbox® • Sounds Like Fun: Phonemic Awareness • TEC60913

Gg
goat
©The Mailbox® • Sounds Like Fun: Phonemic Awareness • TEC60913
Hh
horse
©The Mailbox® • Sounds Like Fun: Phonemic Awareness • TEC60913
Ii
iguana
©The Mailbox® • Sounds Like Fun: Phonemic Awareness • TEC60913

jaguar
Jj
©The Mailbox® • Sounds Like Fun: Phonemic Awareness • TEC60913
K
koala
k
©The Mailbox® • Sounds Like Fun: Phonemic Awareness • TEC60913
Ll
lion
©The Mailbox® • Sounds Like Fun: Phonemic Awareness • TEC60913

Mm
mouse
©The Mailbox® • Sounds Like Fun: Phonemic Awareness • TEC60913
N
newt
n
©The Mailbox® • Sounds Like Fun: Phonemic Awareness • TEC60913
Oo
otter
©The Mailbox® • Sounds Like Fun: Phonemic Awareness • TEC60913

Pp pig

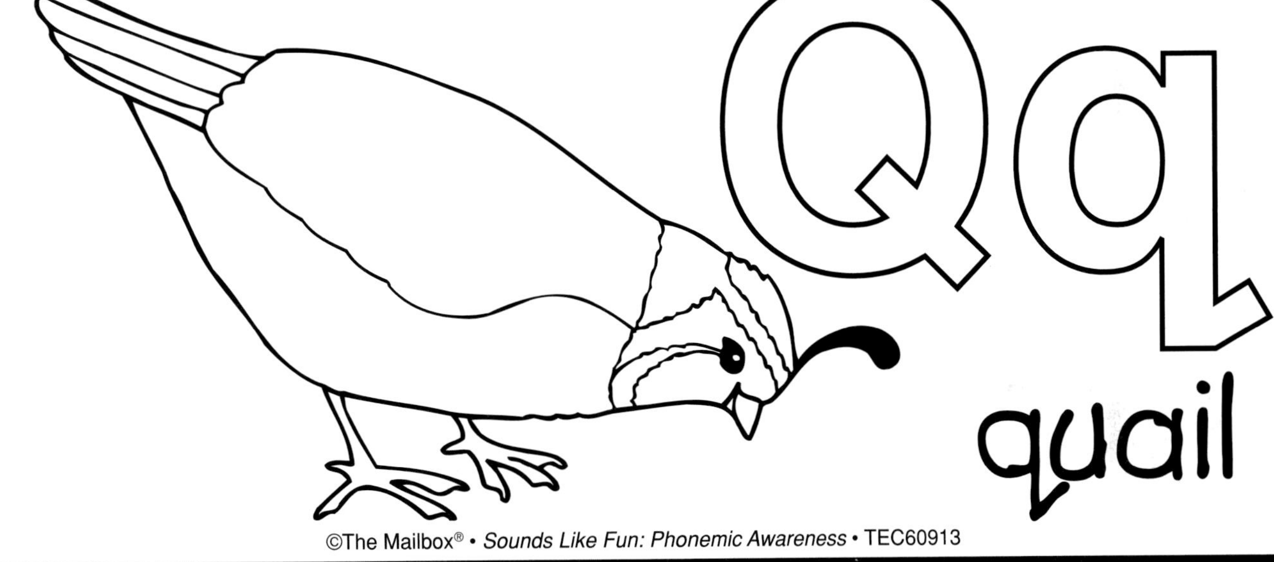

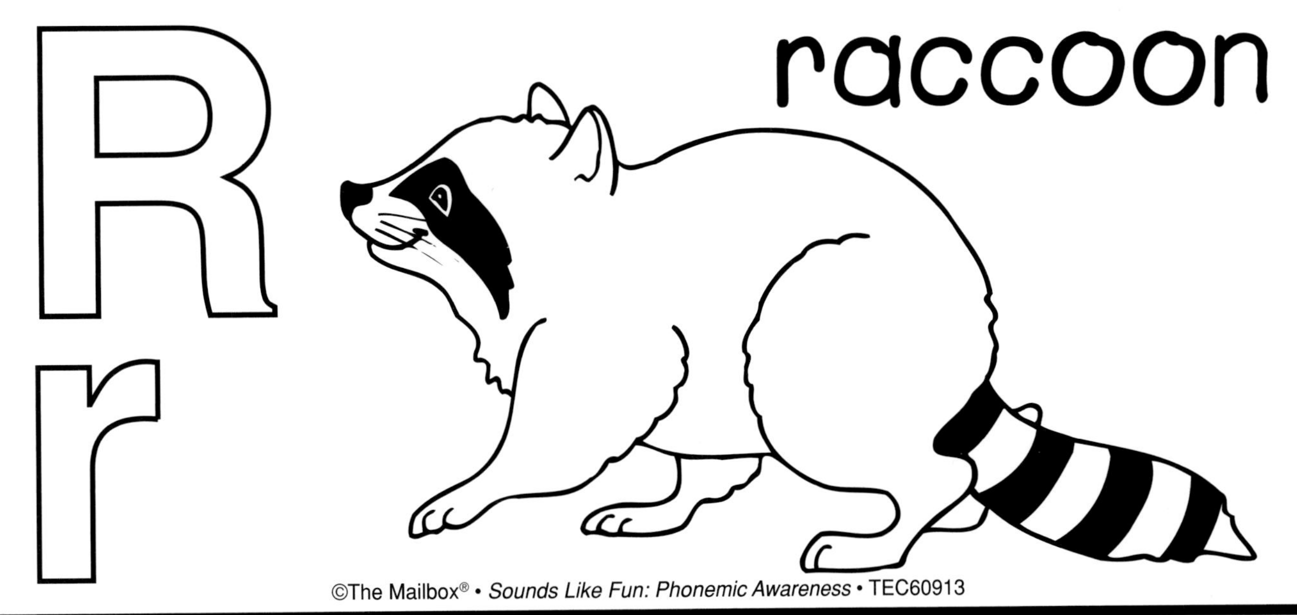

S
seal
s

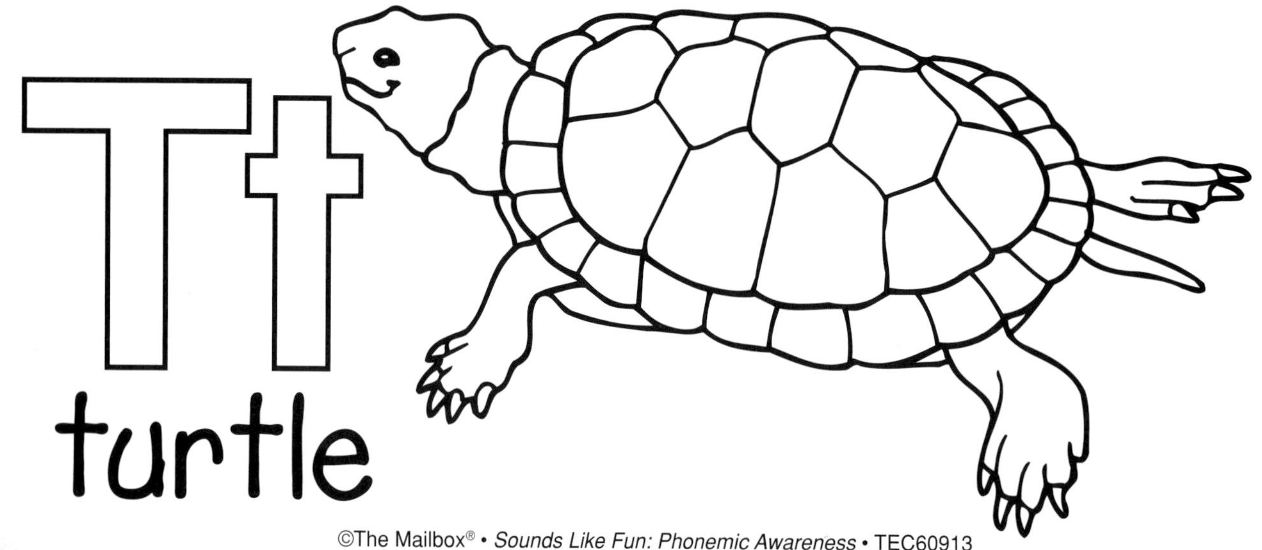
Tt
turtle

Uu
umbrella
cockatoo

Vv
vulture
©The Mailbox® • Sounds Like Fun: Phonemic Awareness • TEC60913
wolf
Ww
©The Mailbox® • Sounds Like Fun: Phonemic Awareness • TEC60913
Xx
x-ray fish
©The Mailbox® • Sounds Like Fun: Phonemic Awareness • TEC60913

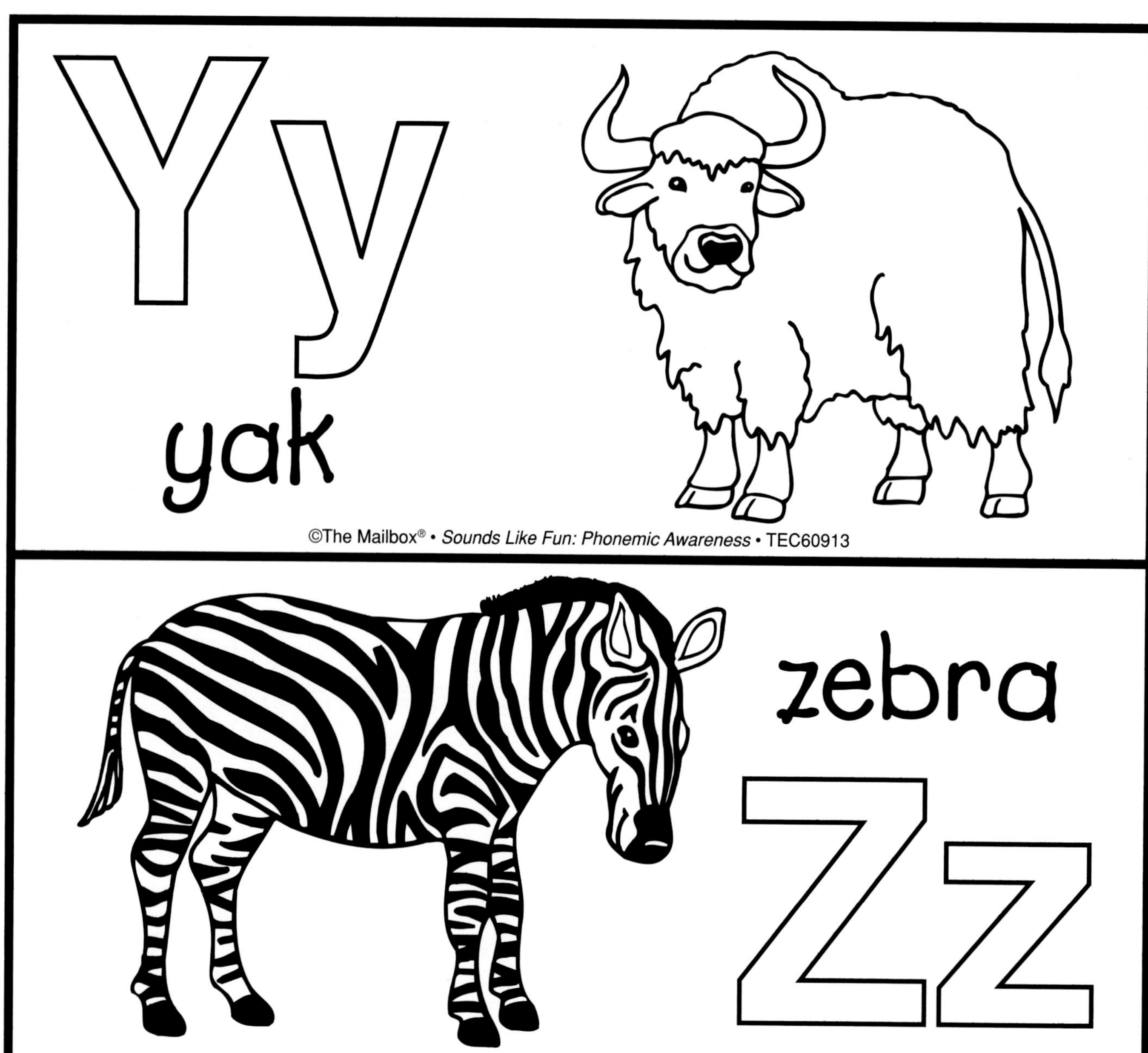
Yy
yak
©The Mailbox® • Sounds Like Fun: Phonemic Awareness • TEC60913
zebra
Zz
©The Mailbox® • Sounds Like Fun: Phonemic Awareness • TEC60913

Ideas, Centers, and Reproducibles

For each consonant and short-vowel sound, this section contains

- inspiring ideas
- a wearable reminder of the sound
- a full-color, center, ready to laminate and ready to use
- a cut-and-paste reproducible

See page 18 to speed your search for a particular sound.

Where to find resources for...

Consonants

Vowels

Sounds Like The Beginning of Bear

The Bear Song

This song will give your ears a real workout. First, to introduce the sound /b/, show the bear miniposter from page 8 and talk with children about the sound they hear at the beginning of the word *bear.* Then teach students the song below and march around together singing it. Afterward, encourage them to think of other words that begin with /b/ and substitute each of those words for *bear* in the verse.

(sung to the tune of "The Farmer in the Dell")

Oh, *bear* begins with /b/.
Oh, *bear* begins with /b/.
Let's use our ears to hear, my friend,
That *bear* begins with /b/.

What's in Bear's Bag?

Curiosity will have your little ones clamoring to see what's in the bag. Draw a simple bear face on a large plain gift bag. Tuck objects that begin with the /b/ sound inside. Include a small ball, a book, a bell, a plush bear, and photos of children whose names begin with the letter *b.* During circle time, show youngsters the bag and explain that it is filled with things whose names begin like *bear.* Remove each item, in turn, for students to name; guide them as they name the object and listen for the /b/ sound. Before placing the bag in a center for similar independent use, add a couple of new *b* objects to it as a surprise.

Bouncing Bear

Get your little bear cubs bouncing with this movement activity. First, show students how to bounce on the balls of their feet, and mention that *bounce* starts with the /b/ sound. Next, recite the chant, bouncing once each time you make the /b/ sound. Then recite the chant with your students as you bounce along together.

I'm a great big bouncing bear.
I bounce here. /B/, /b/, /b/.
I bounce there. /B/, /b/, /b/.

I bounce everywhere I go.
I bounce high. /B/, /b/, /b/.
I bounce low. /B/, /b/, /b/.

I'm so bouncy, don't you know?
I bounce fast. /B/, /b/, /b/.
I bounce slow. /B/.../b/.../b/.

Buzzing Bee Sound

Children love to listen for the /b/ sound when they get to buzz like bees in the process. Gather the picture cards from page 22 or a set of objects, most of which have names that begin with /b/. Hold up each picture or object, in turn, and say its name. Ask students to buzz around in a small circle if they hear /b/ at the beginning of the name. If they don't hear /b/ (and when you've concealed the picture or object), have them silently sit down. Are your ears buzzing too?

Making and Using a Bear Necklace

1. Color the bear and bee.
2. Cut out the pendant and the picture strip along the bold outer lines.
3. Staple the ends of a ¾" x 26" crepe paper streamer strip to make a necklace.
4. Fold the pendant in half, slip the streamer strip inside, and glue the folded paper closed.
5. Name the pictures on the strip, listening for the /b/ sound at the beginning of each word. Glue the strip to the back of the pendant.
6. Find someone with whom to discuss the /b/ sound.

/b/ picture strip

B b

Glue the picture strip here.

Let's talk about words that begin like ***bear*** and ***bee***.

Using These Cards With "Begins Like Bear" on Page 23

1. Before using pages 22 and 23, photocopy pages 21 and 24 for later use.
2. If desired, laminate the center mat (page 23) and the cards.
3. Cut out the cards.
4. To use, have a child place each picture that begins with the /b/ sound on the center mat.
5. Have the child name the pictures on the center, listening to confirm that they all begin like *bear.*

These cards may also be used with "Buzzing Bee Sound" on page 20.

Begins Like Bear

Name________________________________ /b/ sound

Begins Like Bear

Cut.  Glue.

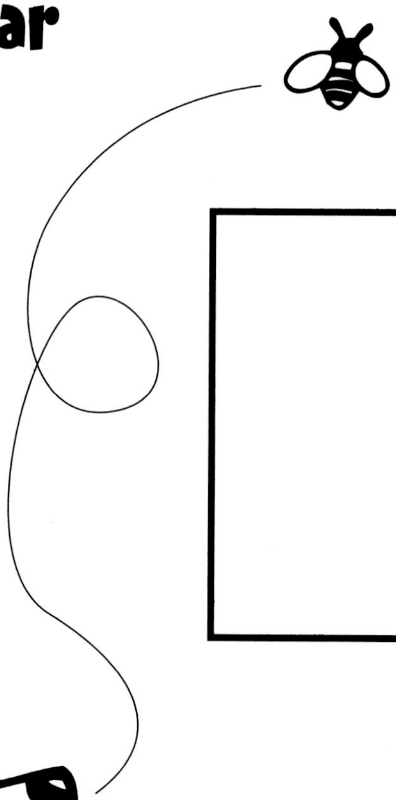

b

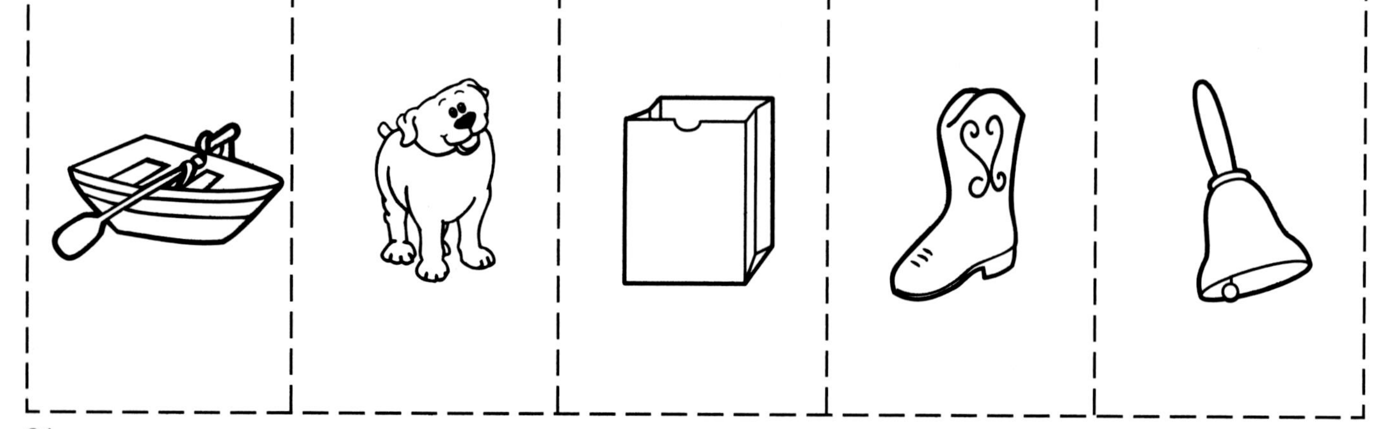

Sounds Like The Beginning of Cat

Catchy Cat Song

Here's a "purr-fectly" catchy cat song for introducing the hard sound of *c.*

(sung to the tune of "Bingo")

There is a critter starts with /k/,
And do you know its name-o?
/K/, /k/, /k/, /k/, cat.
/K/, /k/, /k/, /k/, cat.
/K/, /k/, /k/, /k/, cat.
Oh, yes! Cat is its name-o.

Cuddle the Cat

Your cat fanciers will pounce on the opportunity to cuddle a cat during this phonemic circle game. To begin, seat children in a circle and give a plush cat toy to a child. Then ask him, "Can you cuddle the cat?" emphasizing the /k/ sounds. Invite him to cuddle and stroke the cat as he answers, "Yes, I can. I can cuddle the cat!" Have him make the /k/ sound and pass the toy to the next child in the circle. Repeat the game in this way, encouraging children to join in on the question, until each child has had a chance to cuddle the cat!

Clap for *C*

Applause is guaranteed with this listening game. Gather several easy-to-find items that begin with the hard *c* sound (such as a can, a cap, and a cup). Include a couple of objects in your assortment which do not begin with the /k/ sound. To prepare to play, invite children to turn their listening ears all the way up. Then display one of the objects and have children help you identify it. If the item begins like *cat,* have everyone clap. But if there is no /k/ sound at the beginning, have your little ones hold their applause. Continue with the remainder of your items. When you're done, give your children some applause for their fabulous listening ears.

Copy Cat Can

Your youngsters don't have to be copycats to get a kick out of this action chant. As you say each line, ask children to join in orally and then pantomime each line's ending verb. At long last, it's great to be a copycat!

Copy Cat can catch. /K/, /k/, catch!	*Pretend to catch a ball.*
Copy Cat can cough. /K/, /k/, cough!	*Put hand over mouth; pretend to cough.*
Copy Cat can cover. /K/, /k/, cover!	*Cover eyes with hands.*
Copy Cat can cut. /K/, /k/, cut!	*Make scissors motion with fingers.*
Copy Cat can call. /K/, /k/, call!	*Say, "Meow."*
Now clap, clap, clap for Copy Cat!	*Clap hands.*

©The Mailbox®

Glue the picture strip here.

Note: Some words that have the same beginning sound as *cat* **(/k/) begin with** *c* **and some begin with** *k***. The focus of this activity is on** *c* **words that make the same beginning sound as** *cat***. But** *k* **words like** *kite* **may also be mentioned since they share the beginning sound of** *cat***.**

C
c

Let's talk about words that begin like **cat.**

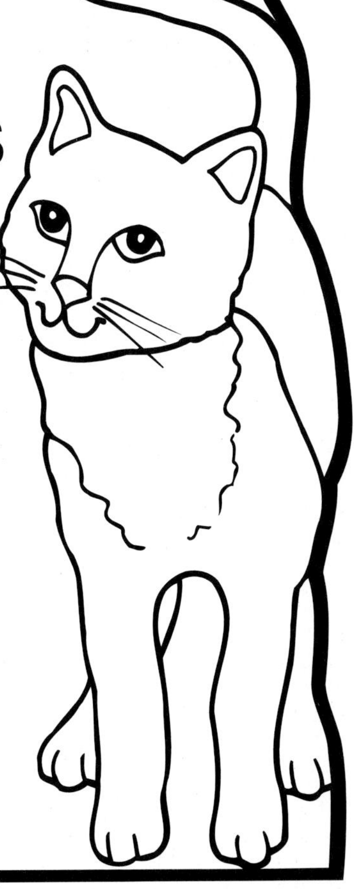

C
c

Making and Using a Cat Necklace

1. Color the cat.
2. Cut out the pendant and the picture strip along the bold outer lines.
3. Staple the ends of a ¾" x 26" crepe paper streamer strip to make a necklace.
4. Fold the pendant in half, slip the streamer strip inside, and glue the folded paper closed.
5. Name the pictures on the picture strip, listening for the /k/ sound at the beginning of each word. Glue the picture strip to the back of the pendant.
6. Find someone with whom to discuss the /k/ sound.

/k/ picture strip

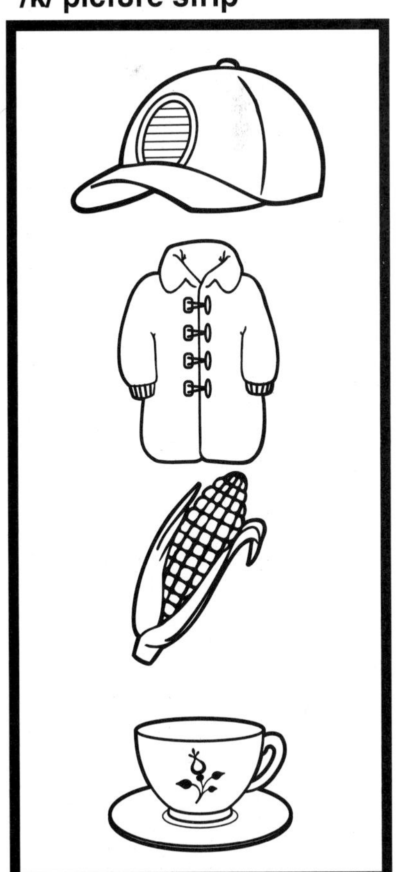

Using These Cards With "Begins Like Cat" on Page 29

1. Before using pages 28 and 29, photocopy pages 27 and 30 for later use.
2. If desired, laminate the center mat (page 29) and the cards.
3. Cut out the cards.
4. To use, have a child place each picture whose name begins with /k/ on the center mat.
5. Have the child name the pictures on the center mat, listening to confirm that they all begin like *cat.*

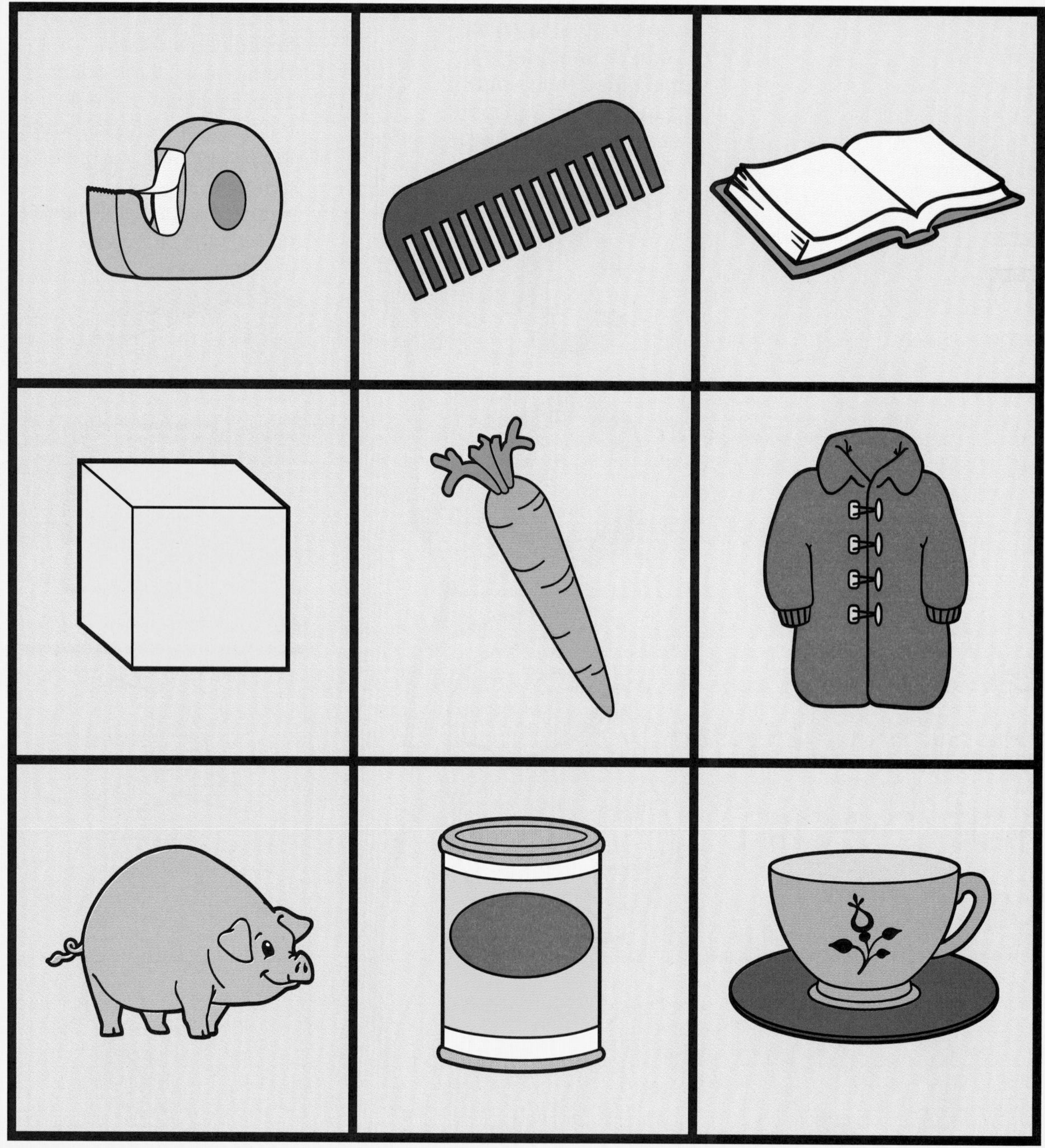

Begins Like Cat

Name____ hard c sound

Begins Like Cat

Cut. Glue.

c

Sounds Like The Beginning of Dog

Listen, Listen

If your children really dig this song about the beginning sound in *dog,* substitute other *d* words in additional verses. Hey! You could feature *dig* in the second verse!

(sung to the tune of "Twinkle, Twinkle, Little Star")

Listen; listen; lend an ear.
Listen; listen; can you hear?
Dog begins with /d/, you know.
Dog begins with /d/, that's so.
Listen; listen; can you hear
/D/, /d/, /d/, /d/ loud and clear?

Hot Diggity Dog!

All your children will be eager to dig up some *d* words—literally. Display several small items whose names begin with /d/ at the sand table. Include things like dominoes, plastic dinosaurs, and dice. Invite a small group of students to take up the doggy habit of digging—have them bury in the sand your *d*-word treasures. Ask them to say the names of the objects, listening for the /d/ sound, before they do. After the objects are well concealed, have another group dig up the items, name them, and listen for the /d/ at the beginning. Choose another small group of children and repeat the activity.

Doggie's Dinner Dish

Place a large plastic dish or new, unbreakable dog dish on the floor for a circle-time game. Help your youngsters brainstorm names of foods that begin like *dog,* such as dates, doughnuts, Danish pastries, and even dill pickles! Begin the activity by saying, "Please put dinner in Doggie's dish," inviting a child volunteer to approach the dish. Have her pretend to put food on the dish as she responds, "I'll put [*d*-word food] in Doggie's dish." Provide assistance with a *d* word if necessary. Continue the game until each child has had a chance to dish up a delightful dinner for Doggie.

D-Word Dance

Isn't *dance* one of the nicest *d* words of all? To prepare for this game, gather the *d* picture cards from page 34. (Include the non-*d* distractor cards if your children are rather skilled with phonemic awareness.) Hold up each card, in turn, and have children name it with you. If the word begins with /d/, let the dancing begin! Don't you just love a good /d/ word?

Making and Using a Dog Headband

1. Color and cut out the headband pattern and ears.
2. Glue the headband to the center of a 3" x 24" strip of bulletin board paper or a sentence strip.
3. Fit the strip to your head; then staple the ends together.
4. Staple or tape the ears to the sides of the headband.
5. Find someone with whom to discuss the /d/ sound.

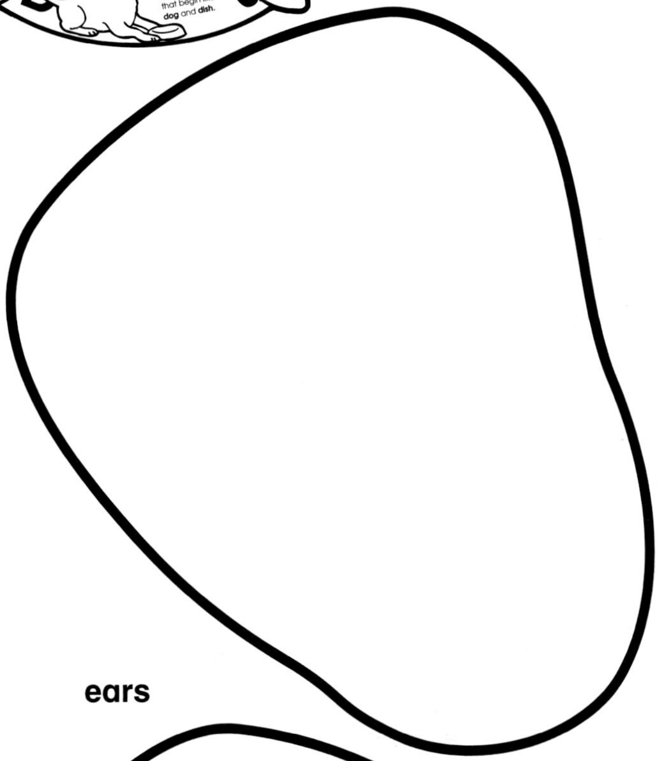

ears

Using These Cards With "Begins Like Dog" on Page 35

1. Before using pages 34 and 35, photocopy pages 33 and 36 for later use.
2. If desired, laminate the center mat (page 35) and the cards.
3. Cut out the cards.
4. To use, have a child place each picture whose name begins with the /d/ sound on the center mat.
5. Have the child name the pictures on the center mat, listening to confirm that they all begin like *dog.*

These cards may also be used with "*D*-Word Dance" on page 32.

Begins Like Dog

Name________________________________ /d/ sound

Begins Like Dog

Cut.

Glue.

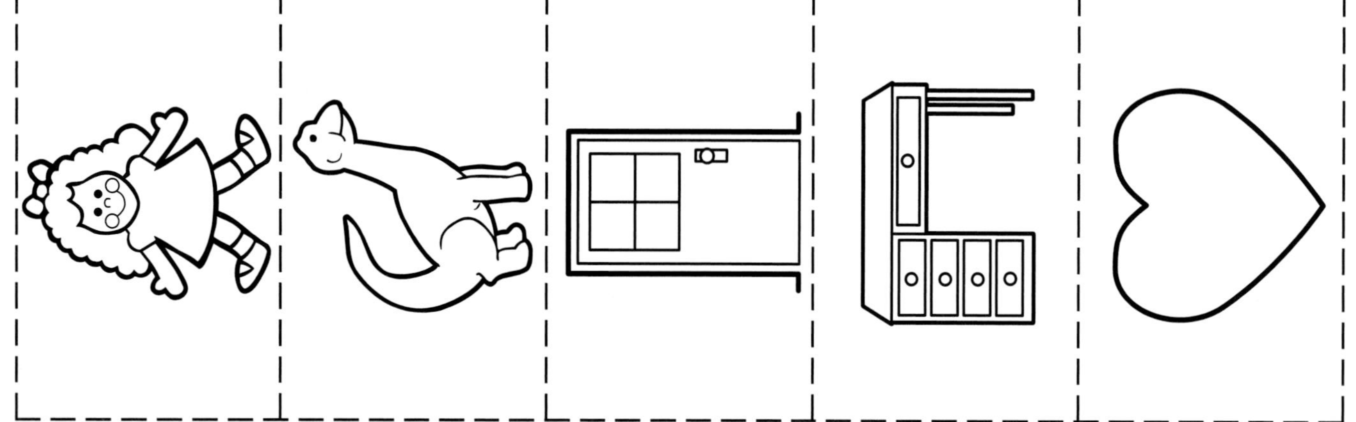

Sounds Like The Beginning of Fox

The Fox Song

You'll feel as sly as a fox when you slip in some phonemic awareness using this familiar tune. After singing this song a time or two, ask your children to think of another word that begins like *fox.* When you've agreed on a word that does, launch into another verse.

(sung to the tune of "London Bridge")

Fox begins with /f/, /f/, /f/.
/F/, /f/, /f/. /F/, /f/, /f/.
Fox begins with /f/, /f/, /f/.
Can you hear it?

Fox Can Find it!

This seek-and-find game is a fun way to reinforce the /f/ sound. To prepare, make a copy of the fox illustration from the center mat on page 41. Mount the fox on tagboard, cut it out, and glue it to a large craft stick to make a stick puppet. Next, gather together easy-to-find items whose names start with *f* such as a feather, a fork, and a football. Scatter the items around the room.

Begin the game by asking, "Who can find a feather?" Hand the fox puppet to a child as you prompt the group to respond, "Fox can find it!" Then have the child help Fox find the feather hidden in the room. Continue in a similar manner with another child searching with Fox for each of the remaining objects. With the collection of items in front of you, have children say all the item names, elongating the /f/ sound for emphasis. Fabulous! All these things that Fox found begin like *fox!*

Follow the Fox

For this follow-the-fox activity, reuse the stick puppet described in "Fox Can Find It!" on page 37. Ahead of time, tape several die-cut 4s and 5s to a large open area of your classroom floor. Then give a student the fox stick puppet and have him lead your students as they march around the numbers, singing this song. As the first verse ends, have each child put his foot near a cutout of the numeral mentioned and keep it there while he sings the next verse. Repeat the song, substituting the word *five* for the word *four.*

(sung to the tune of "The Mulberry Bush")

Follow the fox to find a [four], find a [four], find a [four].
Follow the fox to find a [four]. It's fun to follow Foxie!

Listen to [four] to hear the /f/, to hear the /f/, to hear the /f/.
Listen to [four] to hear the /f/—it's fun to hear the /f/!

A Feather Phenomenon

For this engaging circle-time game, grab a bag of craft feathers and collect some pictures of things whose names begin with *f.* While seated in a circle, show children a feather and a funnel; then talk about the /f/ sound and your supply of pictures. Give each child a feather and ask her to put it on the floor by her foot. Have children pass the funnel around. Randomly call out, "Stop!" Ask the child holding the funnel to say a word that starts with /f/, drop her feather into the funnel, and pass it to the next child. What's that? You want to play again? Okay, but you have to say a different /f/ word this time!

Making and Using a Fox Bracelet

1. Color and cut out the bracelet patterns.
2. Glue the patterns back to back so the pictures show on both sides.
3. Staple the ends together and slip the bracelet on.
4. Find someone with whom to discuss the /f/ sound.

Using These Cards With "Begins Like Fox" on Page 41

1. Before using pages 40 and 41, photocopy pages 39 and 42 for later use.
2. If desired, laminate the center mat (page 41) and the cards.
3. Cut out the cards.
4. To use, have a child place each picture whose name begins with the /f/ sound on the center mat.
5. Have the child name the pictures on the center mat, listening to confirm that they all begin like *fox*.

Begins Like Fox

Name____ /f/ sound

Begins Like Fox

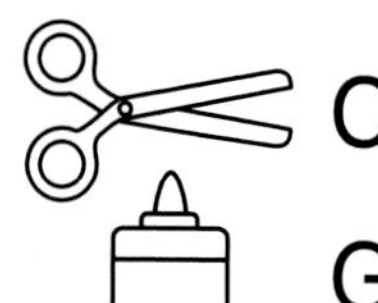

Cut.

Glue.

f

Sounds Like The Beginning of Goat

The Goat Song

Ready to get going with the hard *g* sound? Grab a goat picture, puppet, or stuffed toy. It will become an instant celebrity as you sing this song!

(sung to the tune of "Short'nin' Bread")

Goat begins with /g/. Oh, can you hear it?
Goat begins with /g/, /g/, /g/, /g/, /g/.
/G/: it's a good sound. Say it with me.
/G/: it's a good sound. Yes sirree!

A Gift for a Goat

You will need a large, sturdy gift box and an assortment of items (such as gum, a game, and a plastic gorilla) or pictures whose names begin with the hard *g* sound. Display the items or pictures on a table. To begin, talk with your children about the beginning sound in *gift* and *goat* and ask them to help you choose some gifts for a goat that begin with /g/. Next, hold up each item or picture, in turn, and say its name. If the name begins with /g/, prompt students to respond by saying, "A [*g* word] is a gift for a goat," and place it inside the gift box. If the item does not begin with /g/, have children say, "A [non-*g* word] is not a gift for a goat." Later, place the gift box and *g* items in a center for independent student use.

Goat's Guessing Game

Challenge students to guess the *g* word that completes each sentence. Cut out the headband from a copy of page 45. As you display the headband, ask children to recall the beginning sound of *goat.* Then ask that they listen to the following sentences and think of words that begin with /g/ to complete them.

When a goat or a horse runs, it _____. *(gallops)*

A goat can eat weeds and _____. *(garbage)*

To a goat, butting heads may be a _____. *(game)*

To keep a goat out of the yard, close the _____. *(gate)*

You might need a fence to keep a goat out of your _____. *(garden)*

G-G-Goat!

Vary the game Duck, Duck, Goose to help children practice saying and hearing the hard *g* sound. Ask your little ones to sit in a circle. Select one child to be the goat. Have him wear a goat headband you've made using page 45. As the child walks around the outside of the circle, direct him to say the /g/ sound instead of "duck" as he taps classmates' heads. Have him say, "Goat!" when he taps the head of the child who will stand up and chase him around the circle. Not since the three billy goats Gruff tricked the troll have you seen kids hightail it like that!

Making and Using a Goat Headband

1. Color and cut out the headband and horns.
2. Glue the headband to the center of a 3" x 24" strip of bulletin board paper or a sentence strip.
3. Fit the strip to your head; then staple the ends together.
4. Staple or tape the horns to the sides of the headband.
5. Find someone with whom to discuss the /g/ sound.

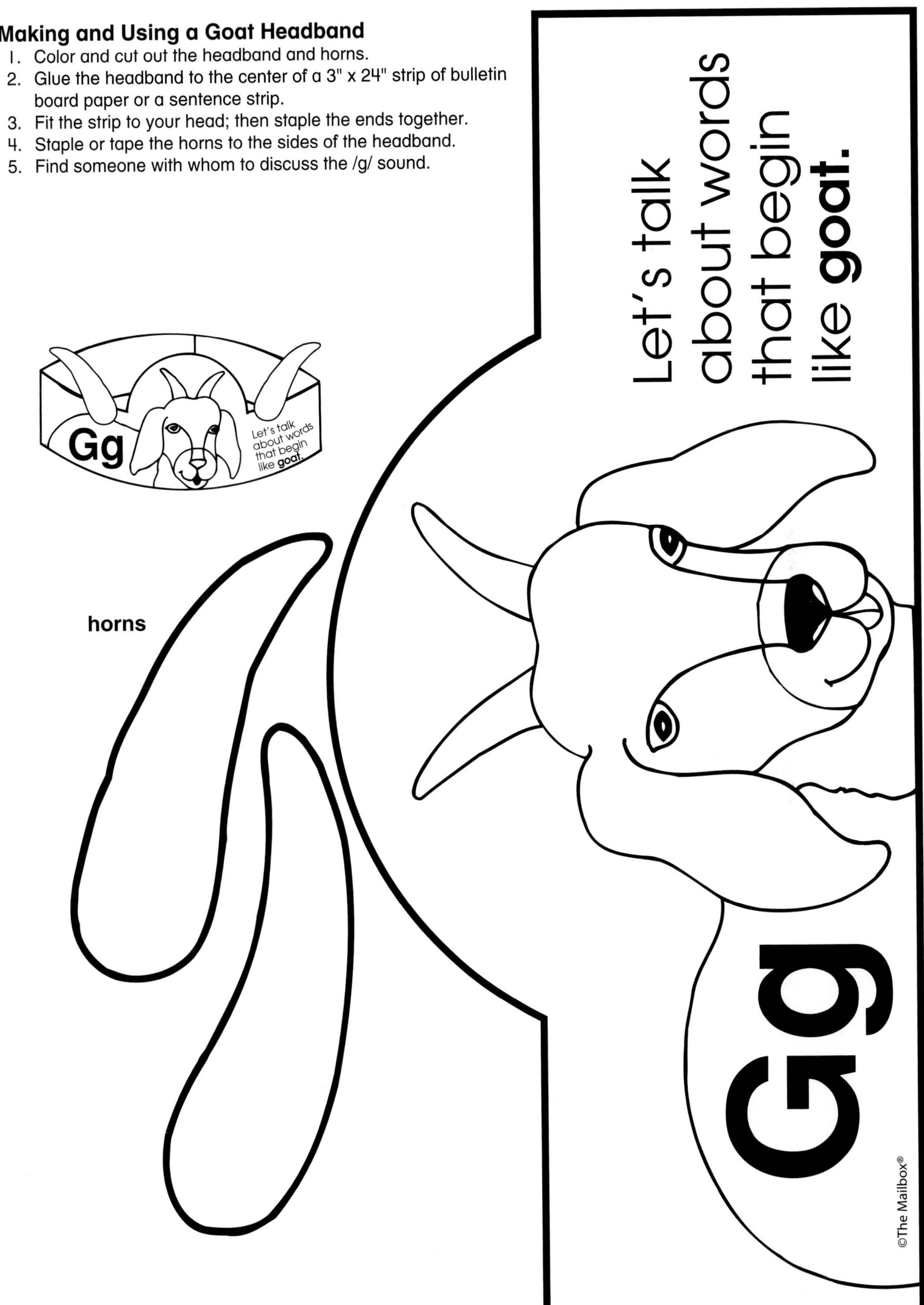

Using These Cards With "Begins Like Goat" on Page 47

1. Before using pages 46 and 47, photocopy pages 45 and 48 for later use.
2. If desired, laminate the center mat (page 47) and the cards.
3. Cut out the cards.
4. To use, have a child place each picture whose name begins with the /g/ sound on the center mat.
5. Have the child name the pictures on the center mat, listening to confirm that they all begin like *goat.*

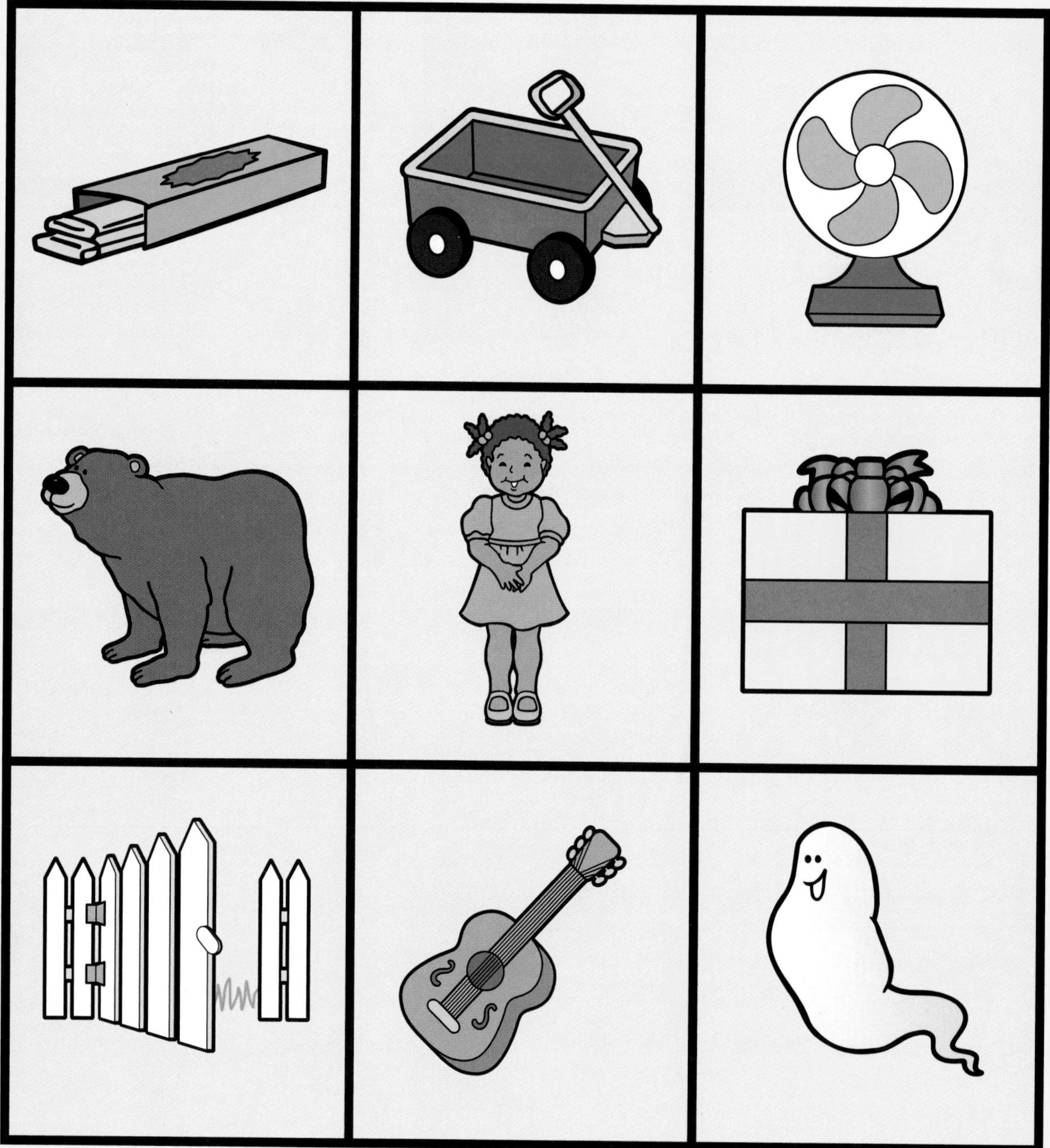

Begins Like Goat

Name____

Begins Like Goat

Cut.

Glue.

Sounds Like The Beginning of Horse

Horsing Around

Help little ones become familiar with the /h/ sound with this happy tune.

(sung to the tune of "The Farmer in the Dell")

Oh, *horse* begins with /h/.
Oh, *horse* begins with /h/.
Let's use our ears to hear, my dears,
That *horse* begins with /h/.

Horsey, Horsey, Do You Hear /H/?

Use strands of crumpled tissue paper hay and copies of the picture cards on page 52 for this activity. To begin, discuss the /h/ sound at the beginning of *horse* and *hay.* Have three children pretend to be horses as they stand behind a long table facing their classmates. Place some tissue paper hay in front of each child. Explain that you will put a picture card in each pile of hay and that each child will decide whether the picture's name starts with /h/ as in *horse* and *hay.* When children have made up their minds, chant with the audience, "Horsey, Horsey, do you hear /h/?" Each child responds in turn. If the child does not have a word that begins with /h/, he says no. If he does have an *h* word, have him say, "/H/, /h/, [name of his picture]." Continue playing until every child has had a turn being a horse.

The Horsey Hokey-Pokey

When you and your youngsters do this version of the Hokey-Pokey, you may want to draw the blinds. We wouldn't want people to think you were just horsing around! Discuss the beginning sound of *horse.* Then explain that you'll be singing "The Horsey Hokey-Pokey" and including some other *h* words: *hoof, hip,* and *head!* Here we go!

You put your [right hoof] here.
You put your [right hoof] there.
You put your [right hoof] here,
And you shake it in the air.
Do the horsey Hokey-Pokey
And turn yourself around.
/H/, /h/. /H/, /h/, /h/, /h/!

Repeat the verse, replacing the underlined words with left hoof, right hip, left hip, *and* head right.

What's Under Horsey's Hay?

Turn your sensory table into a hayrack for hands-on exploration. Put some paper hearts, toy hammers, party hats, toy horns, and plastic clothes hangers in the table. Then cover the items with crumpled tissue paper strips to resemble hay. Invite a small group of students to find each item under the hay, say its name, and make the /h/ sound. Once all of the items have been found, ask children to hide them under the hay for the next group to find.

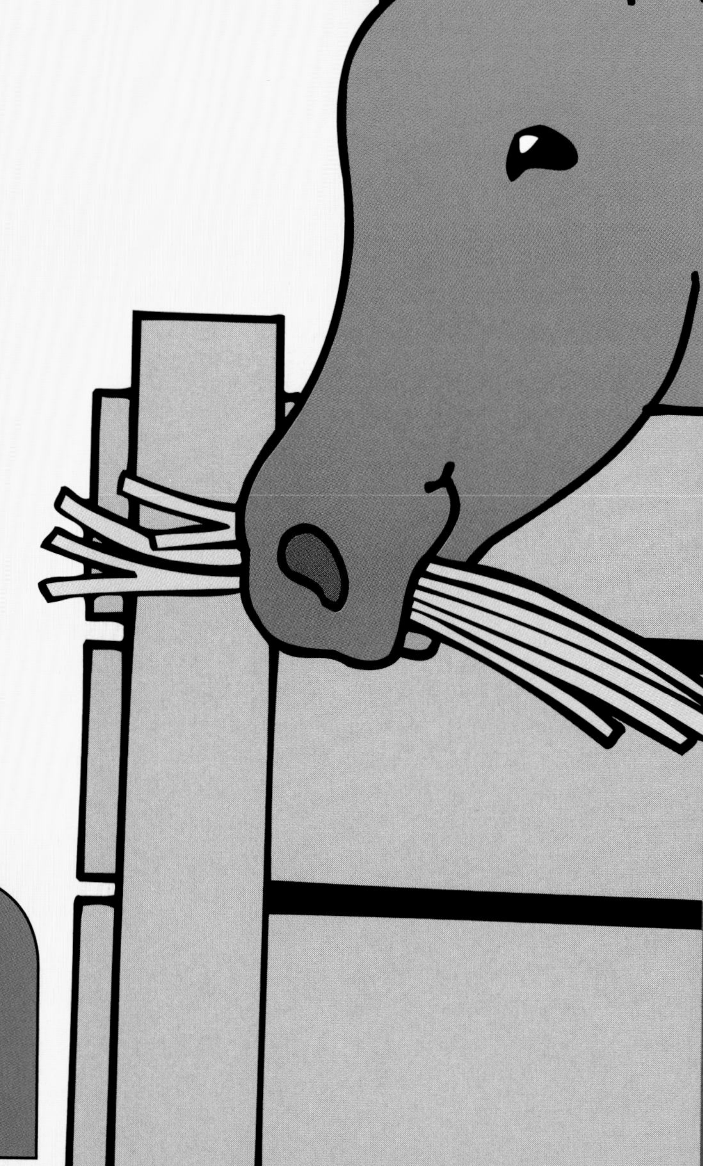

Hh

Making and Using a Horse Necklace

1. Color the horse.
2. Cut out the pendant and the picture strip along the bold outer lines.
3. Staple the ends of a ¾" x 26" crepe paper streamer strip to make a necklace.
4. Fold the pendant in half, slip the streamer strip inside, and glue the folded paper closed.
5. Name the pictures on the picture strip, listening for the /h/ sound at the beginning of each word. Glue the picture strip to the back of the pendant.
6. Find someone with whom to discuss the /h/ sound.

Let's talk about words that begin like horse.

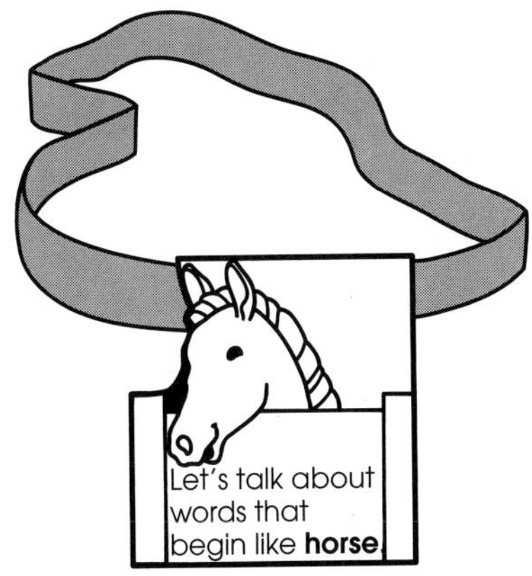

/h/ picture strip

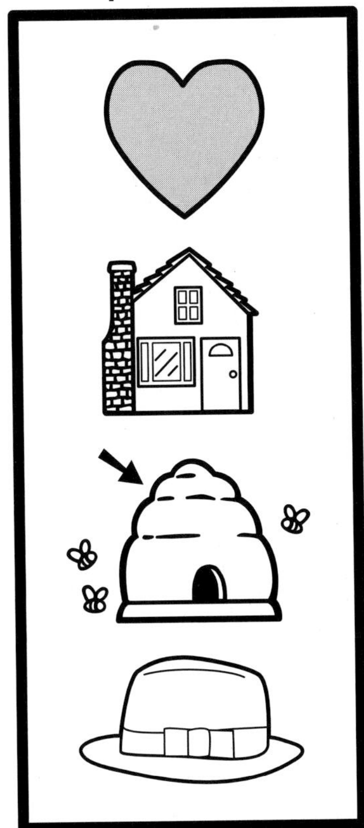

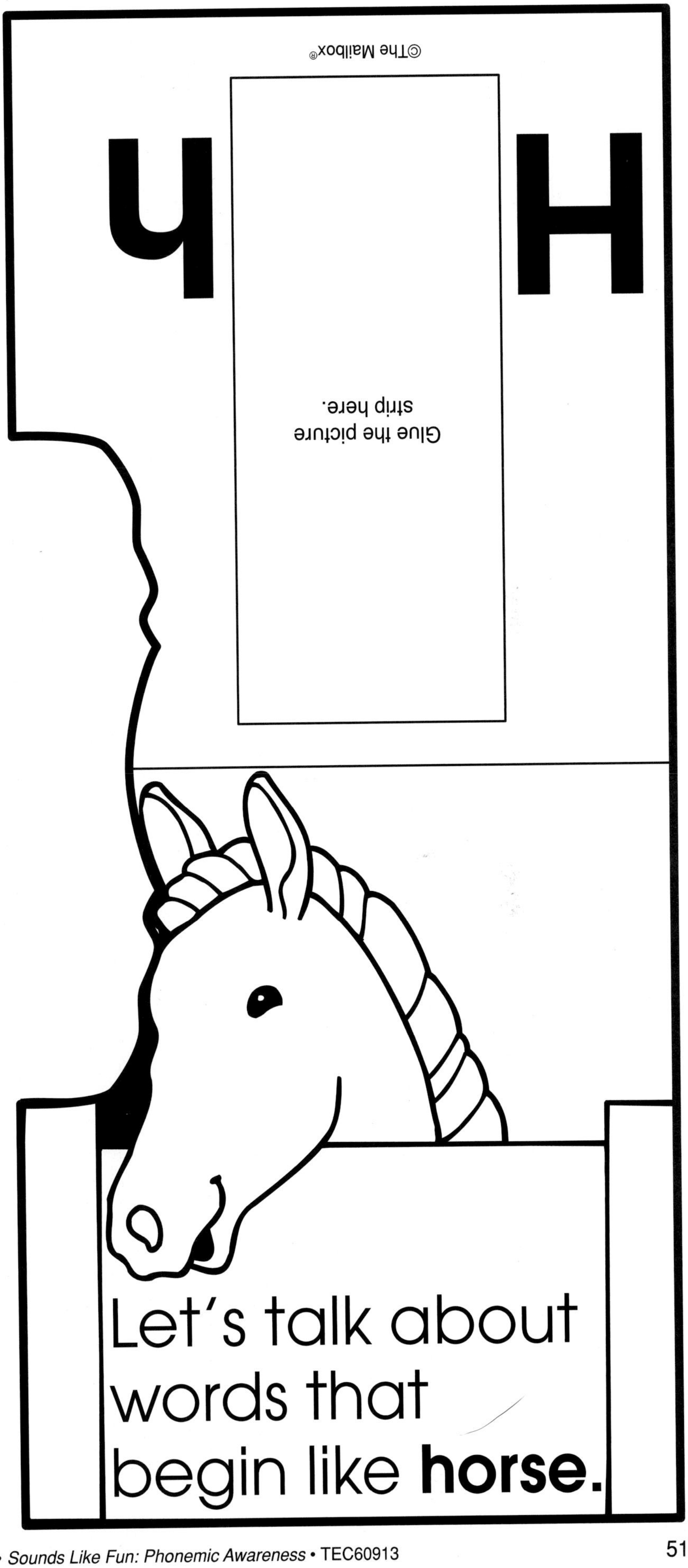
©The Mailbox®
h
H
Glue the picture strip here.
Let's talk about words that begin like **horse.**

Using These Cards With "Begins Like Horse" on Page 53

1. Before using pages 52 and 53, photocopy pages 51 and 54 for later use.
2. If desired, laminate the center mat (page 53) and the cards.
3. Cut out the cards.
4. To use, have a child place each picture whose name begins with the /h/ sound on the center mat.
5. Have the child name the pictures on the center mat, listening to confirm that they all begin like *horse*.

These cards may also be used with "Horsey, Horsey, Do You Hear /H/?" on page 49.

Begins Like Horse

Name________________________________ /h/ sound

Begins Like Horse

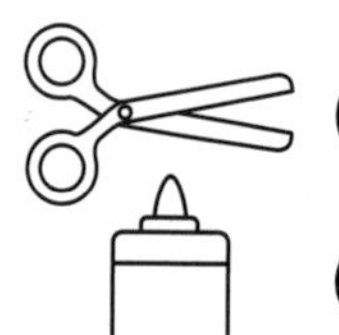

Cut.

Glue.

h

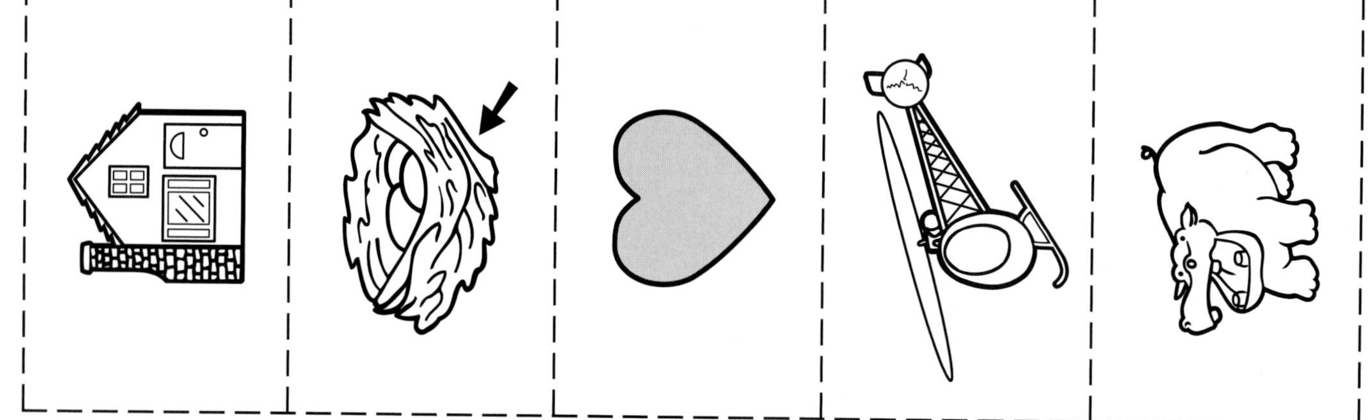

Sounds Like The Beginning of Jaguar

Jaguar Song

Get the jump on phonemic awareness with this jazzy jaguar tune.

(sung to the tune of "Are You Sleeping?")

Jaguar, jaguar,
Jaguar, jaguar
Starts with /j/,
Starts with /j/.
Come on, now let's say it.
Come on, now let's say it.
/J/, /j/, /j/. /J/, /j/, /j/.

Jaguar's Jar

There'll be no snarling or growling while playing this jaguar game! You will need a jumbo wide-mouthed plastic jar and small items (such as a toy jeep, a jump rope, and some jacks) or pictures representing words that begin with /j/ (see page 58). Display the items or pictures along with a few others that do not start with /j/. To begin, ask students to help you choose some things for Jaguar's jar, selecting only things with names that begin like *jaguar*. Next, hold up each item, in turn, and say its name. If the item begins with /j/, prompt students to respond by saying, "Put the [*j* word] in Jaguar's jar." Then place it inside the jar. If the item does not begin with /j/, coach them to say, "Don't put the [non-*j* word] in Jaguar's jar." Later, place the jumbo jar and the items or pictures in a center for independent student use.

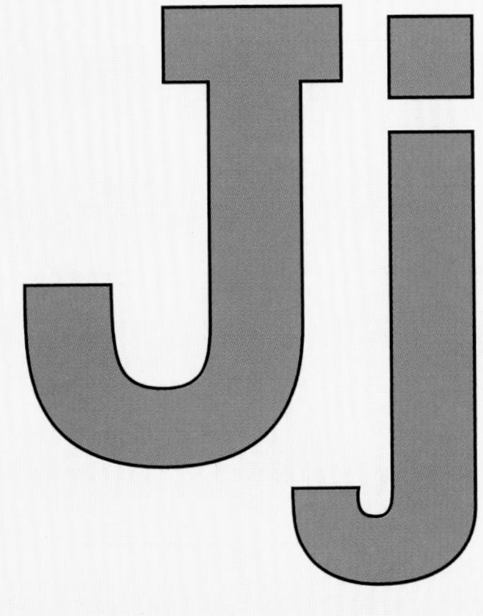

Jaguar Jump

Your little ones will jump at the chance to take part in this movement activity. Recite the chant, jumping once each time you make the /j/ sound. Then recite the chant with your students as you jump together.

I'm a jaguar. Watch me jump.
I jump where it's flat. /J/, /j/, /j/.
I jump over a bump. /J/, /j/, /j/.

I jump everywhere I go.
I jump up high. /J/, /j/, /j/.
I jump down low. /J/, /j/, /j/.

I'm so jumpy, don't you know?
I jump real fast. /J/, /j/, /j/.
I jump so slow. /J/.../j/.../j/.

On the Prowl

In this variation on Musical Chairs, your youngsters get to be big cats prowling around in search of words that begin like *jaguar.* To prepare for the game, make a copy of the picture cards on page 58 and cut them out. Place two groups of four chairs back-to-back as you would for the game of Musical Chairs. Tape the six /j/ cards and two of the other cards to separate chairs. Then invite six children to play the game. Have students circle the chairs, watchfully prowling like jaguars as you play rhythmic music. Encourage them to softly make the /j/ sound to the beat of the tune as they prowl. When you stop the music, challenge players to find a chair that features a /j/ picture word and sit down. Talk about the names of the pictures they choose, and switch a few chairs around before sending them on the prowl again!

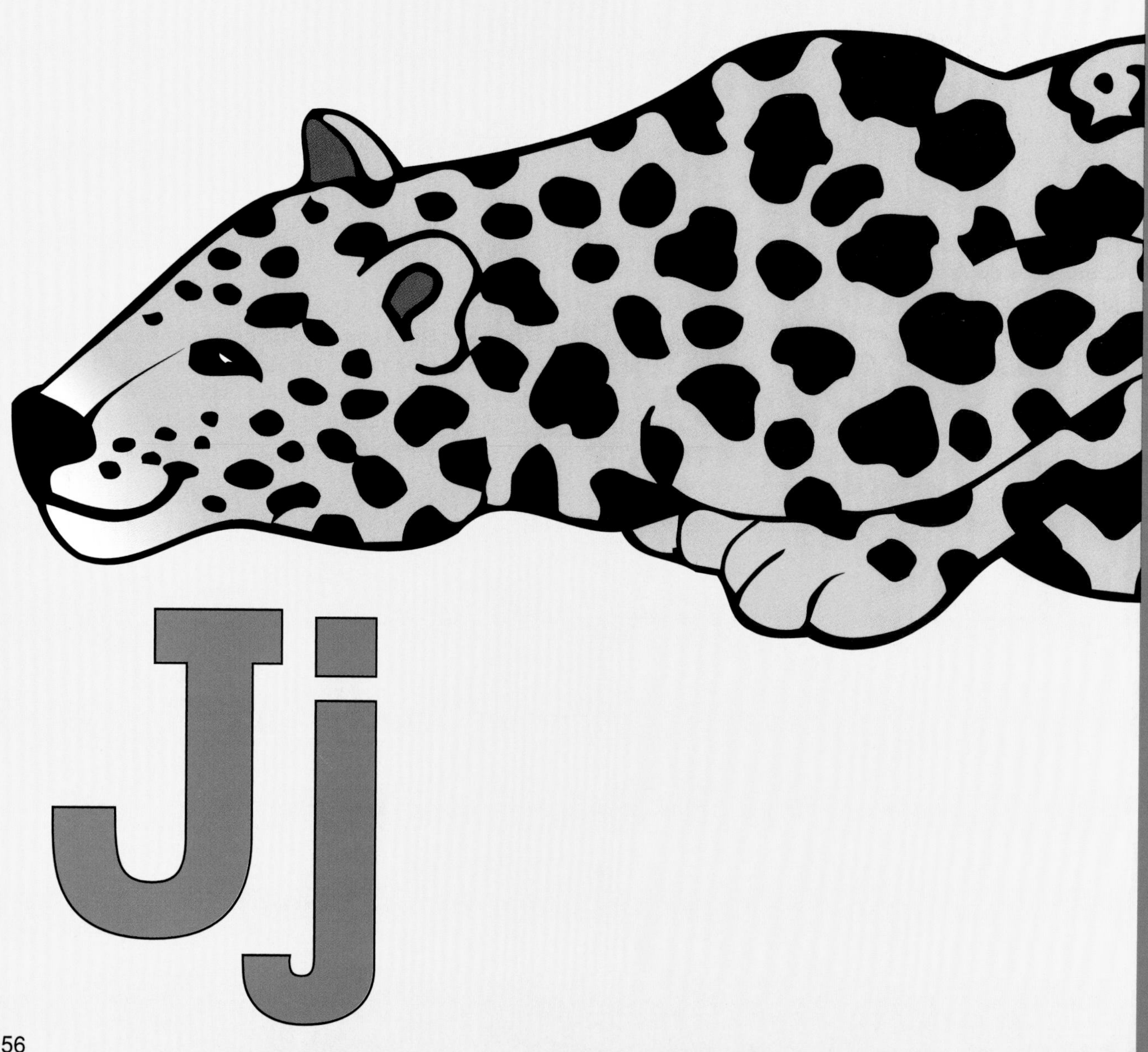

Making and Using a Jaguar Bracelet

1. Color and cut out the bracelet patterns.
2. Glue the patterns back-to-back so the pictures show on both sides.
3. Staple the ends together and slip the bracelet on.
4. Find someone with whom to discuss the /j/ sound.

Using These Cards With "Begins Like Jaguar" on Page 59

1. Before using pages 58 and 59, photocopy pages 57 and 60 for later use.
2. If desired, laminate the center mat (page 59) and the cards.
3. Cut out the cards.
4. To use, have each child place each picture whose name begins with the /j/ sound on the center mat.
5. Have the child name the pictures on the center mat, listening to confirm that they all begin like *jaguar.*

These cards may also be used with "Jaguar's Jar" on page 55 and "On the Prowl" on page 56.

Begins Like Jaguar

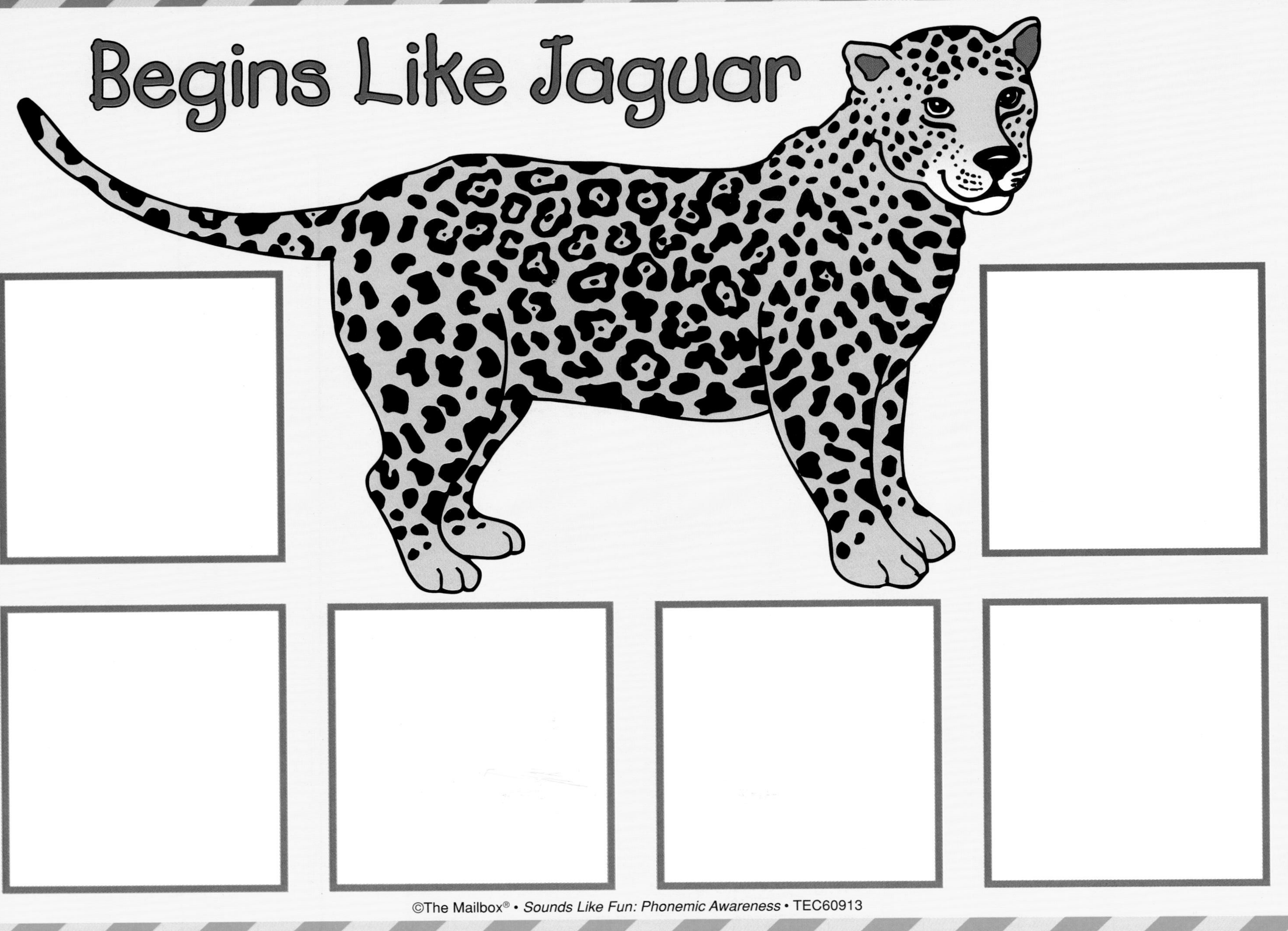

Name____ /j/ sound

Begins Like Jaguar

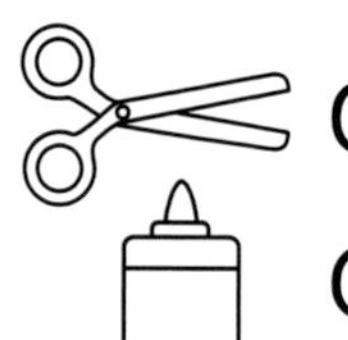

Cut.

Glue.

j

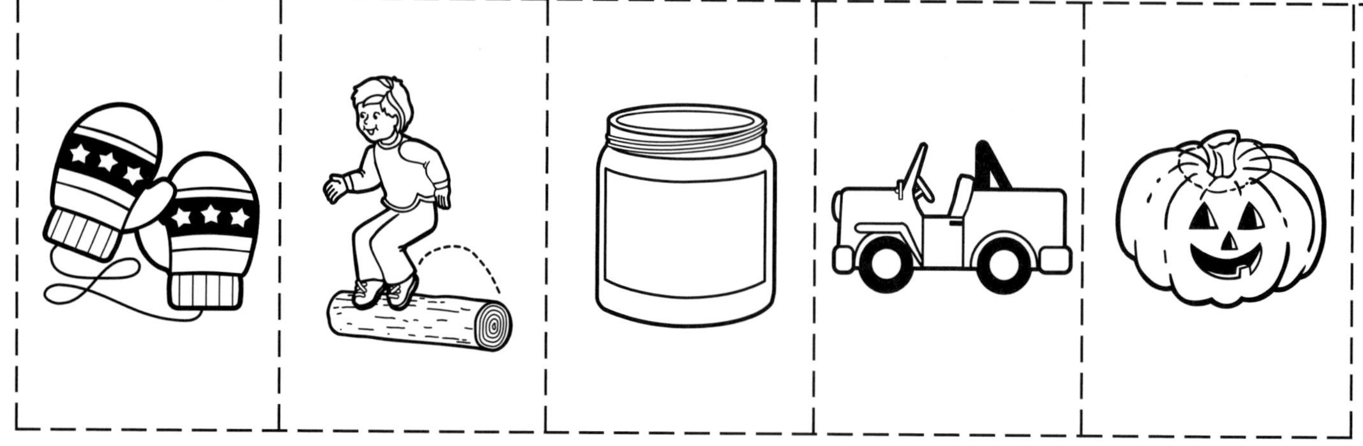

Sounds Like The Beginning of Koala

The Koala Song

This familiar movement tune can now become a favorite phonemic awareness song. Talk with your children about the sound heard at the beginning of *koala;* then sing this song.

(sung to the tune of "The Wheels on the Bus")

Koala is a critter that starts with /k/,
/K/, /k/, /k/. /K/, /k/, /k/.
Koala is a critter that starts with /k/.
Say it with me.

Koala Keeps It

Reinforce the sound of /k/ with this group activity. You will need a large plastic Halloween kettle or a large black paper kettle shape glued to a box. Gather together a large key, a die-cut kite shape, an empty plastic ketchup bottle, a kerchief, and pictures of a king and a kitten. Display the items on a table along with a bag, a toy truck, and a spoon. To begin, discuss the beginning sound in *koala* and ask students to help you choose some things that a koala can keep. Tell them that they may only select things that begin like *koala.* Next, hold up each item, in turn, and say its name. If the item begins with /k/, prompt students to respond by saying, "Koala keeps a [*k* word]," and then place it inside the kettle. If the item does not begin with /k/, have them say, "Koala can't keep a [non-*k* word]." Later, place the kettle and the items in a center for independent use.

Koala Can Kick

Everyone will get a kick out of this movement poem, especially if they're all wearing their koala headbands (page 63) as they move! Encourage youngsters to listen carefully for the beginning sound of the words *koala* and *kick.* After saying both verses, talk about the /k/ sound again and discuss the fact that that sneaky /k/ sound can be heard at the end of *trick* and *kick.* /K/ is everywhere!

I'm a koala. I can kick.	*Point to self and kick right foot.*
Watch me kick; it's quite a trick!	*Kick left foot.*
Kick down low	*Do a low kick with right foot.*
And kick up high.	*Do a high kick with left foot.*
/K/, /k/, kick up to the sky!	*Do a high kick with right foot.*

I'm a koala. I can kick.	*Point to self and kick each foot in turn.*
Watch me kick; it's quite a trick!	*Kick each foot in turn.*
Kick over here	*Kick left foot across right foot.*
And kick over there.	*Kick right foot across left foot.*
/K/, /k/, kick up in the air!	*Kick each foot, in turn, high in the air.*

Koala, Koala, Do You Have a Key?

The key to beginning-sound fun is this version of the traditional game Button, Button, Who Has the Button? To begin, tell several children that they are going to be koalas standing in a line facing an audience of classmates. Talk about the beginning sound of *koala* and have them determine whether *koala* and *key* begin with the same sound. Ask them to extend their hands palm to palm as in the traditional game. Then secretly pass keys to some of the koalas. Prompt the audience to find the keys by asking each child, in turn, "Koala, Koala, do you have a k-k-key?" If the child does not have a key, have him shake his head no three times as he makes the /k/ sound. If he does have a key, have him nod his head yes three times as he makes the /k/ sound.

Making and Using a Koala Headband

1. Color and cut out the headband and ears.
2. Glue the headband to the center of a 3" x 24" strip of bulletin board paper or a sentence strip.
3. Fit the strip to your head; then staple the ends together.
4. Staple or tape the ears to the sides of the headband.
5. Find someone with whom to discuss the /k/ sound.

Using These Cards With "Begins Like Koala" on Page 65

1. Before using pages 64 and 65, photocopy pages 63 and 66 for later use.
2. If desired, laminate the center mat (page 65) and the cards.
3. Cut out the cards.
4. To use, have a child place each picture whose name begins with the /k/ sound on the center mat.
5. Have the child name the pictures on the center mat, listening to confirm that they all begin like *koala.*

Begins Like Koala

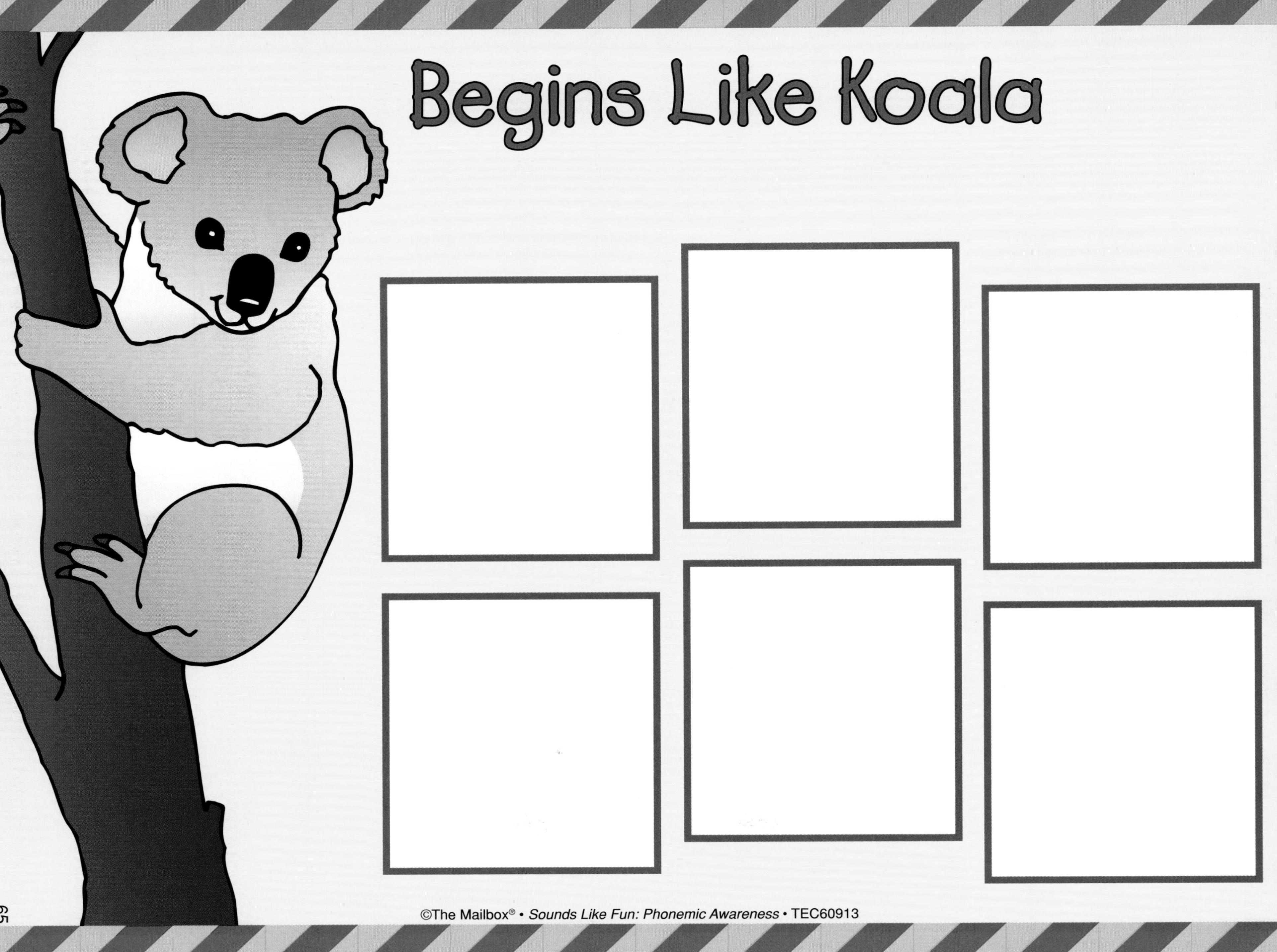

Name____ /k/ sound

Begins Like Koala

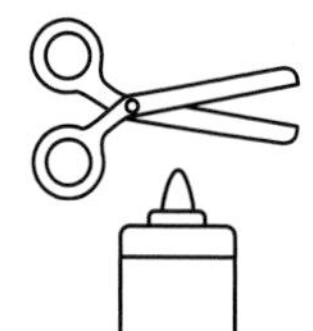

Cut.

Glue.

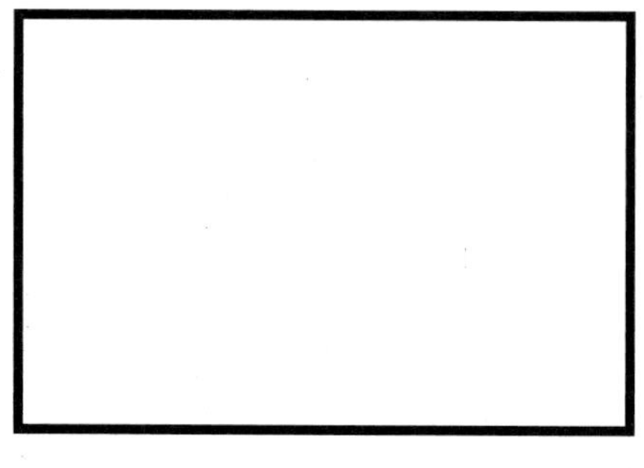

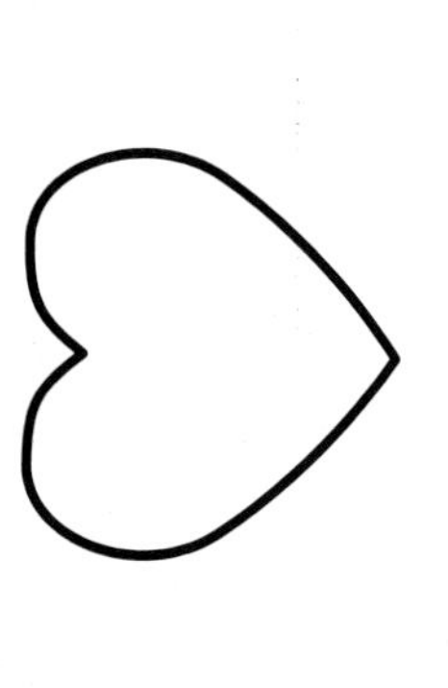

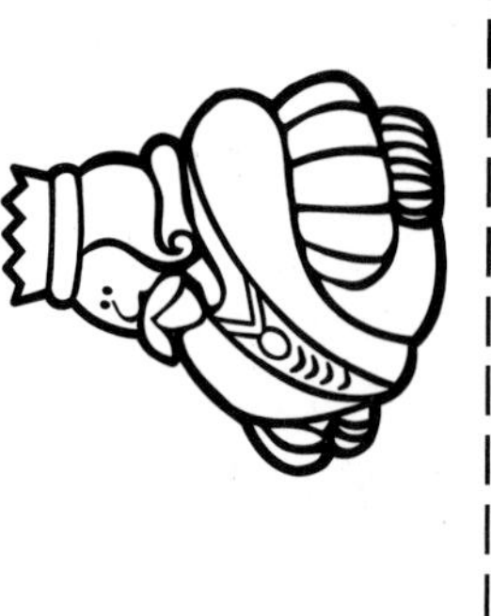

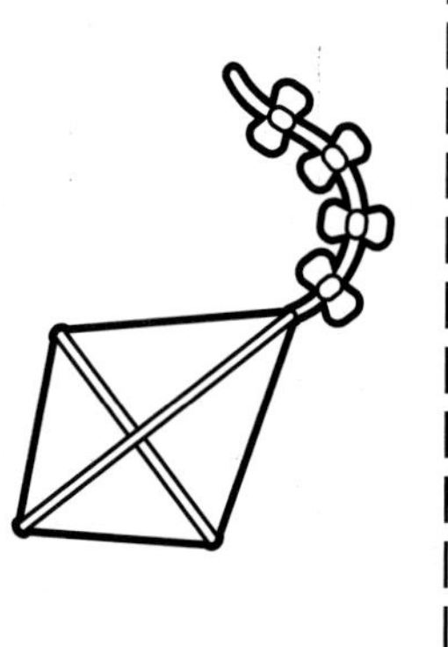

Sounds Like The Beginning of Lion

The Lion Song

Get the lion's share of your youngsters' attention with this tranquil little lion ditty.

(sung to the tune of "Twinkle, Twinkle, Little Star")

/L/, /l/, lions far and near.
Listen carefully, my dear.
/L/, /l/, /l/—it sounds just so.
/L/, /l/, /l/, /l/—now we know.
/L/, /l/, lions prowling round.
Can you hear the /l/, /l/ sound?

In the Lion's Paw

Kids will pounce at the chance to be the lion in this beginning-sound game. To prepare, locate some furry or colorful adult-size gloves that will serve well as lion paws. Also place on a tabletop some items that begin with *l* (such as a lunchbox, a leaf, a lock, a lemon, a lollipop, and a list) and a couple that begin with a different sound.

To begin, ask for a volunteer to be the lion. As her classmates sing "The Lion Song" from this page, have the volunteer put on the lion paws and slink around the table, scanning it for things that begin with /l/. When the verse ends, have the lion scoop up an object that begins with /l/. Provide assistance as needed. Have her say the word to classmates and explain how she knows it starts like *lion.* Continue in the same manner, giving several other children opportunities to be the lion.

Leaping Lions

Listening before leaping is a very important goal in this game. Gather the picture cards from page 70. Have a small group of youngsters stand together on one side of an outstretched jump rope placed on the floor. Explain that they are lions listening for other words that start like *lion.* Hold up a card and say its picture's name and *lion,* emphasizing the initial sounds. Invite your youngsters to leap like a lion to the other side of the rope if both words start with /l/. Remind little ones to take care before they leap—not all the picture words start with /l/. This job of listening can be a very tricky thing!

Roaring Good /l/ Words

Now this is /l/ sound practice your kids will really roar about! Read one of the incomplete sentences below during circle time. When a child suggests a word to complete the sentence, discuss his response with the group. If the group thinks the answer starts with /l/ and is correct, have the whole pride stand up and give a big roar before settling back down in silence. Continue reading and completing sentences and roaring about /l/ words until each sentence has been used. Whew! Roaring is exhausting!

A baby lion isn't big; it's _____. *(little)*
A lion lays around when it's feeling ______. *(lazy)*
A lion cleans its fur by _____. *(licking)*
Lions can jump or ______. *(leap)*
A father lion isn't small; it's _____. *(large)*
If you took a lion for a walk, you'd need a pretty strong _____. *(leash)*

Making and Using a Lion Necklace

1. Color the lion.
2. Cut out the pendant and the picture strip along the bold outer lines.
3. Staple the ends of a ¾" x 26" crepe paper streamer strip to make a necklace.
4. Fold the pendant in half, slip the streamer strip inside, and glue the folded paper closed.
5. Name the pictures on the picture strip, listening for the /l/ sound at the beginning of each word. Glue the picture strip to the back of the necklace.
6. Find someone with whom to discuss /l/ words.

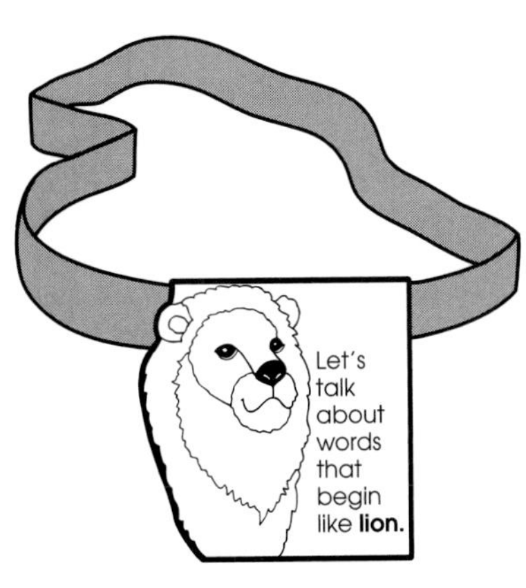

Let's talk about words that begin like **lion.**

/l/ picture strip

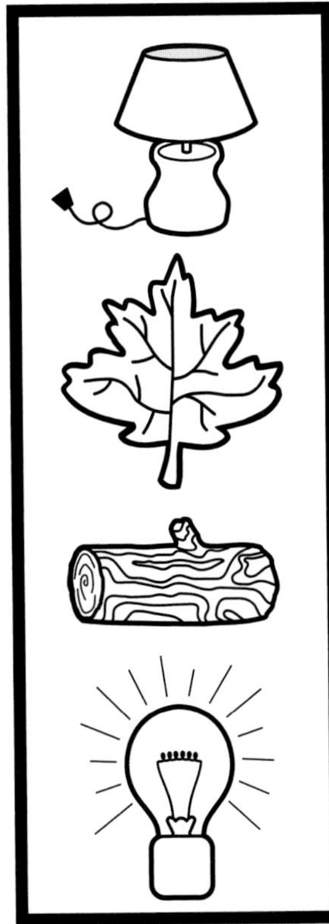

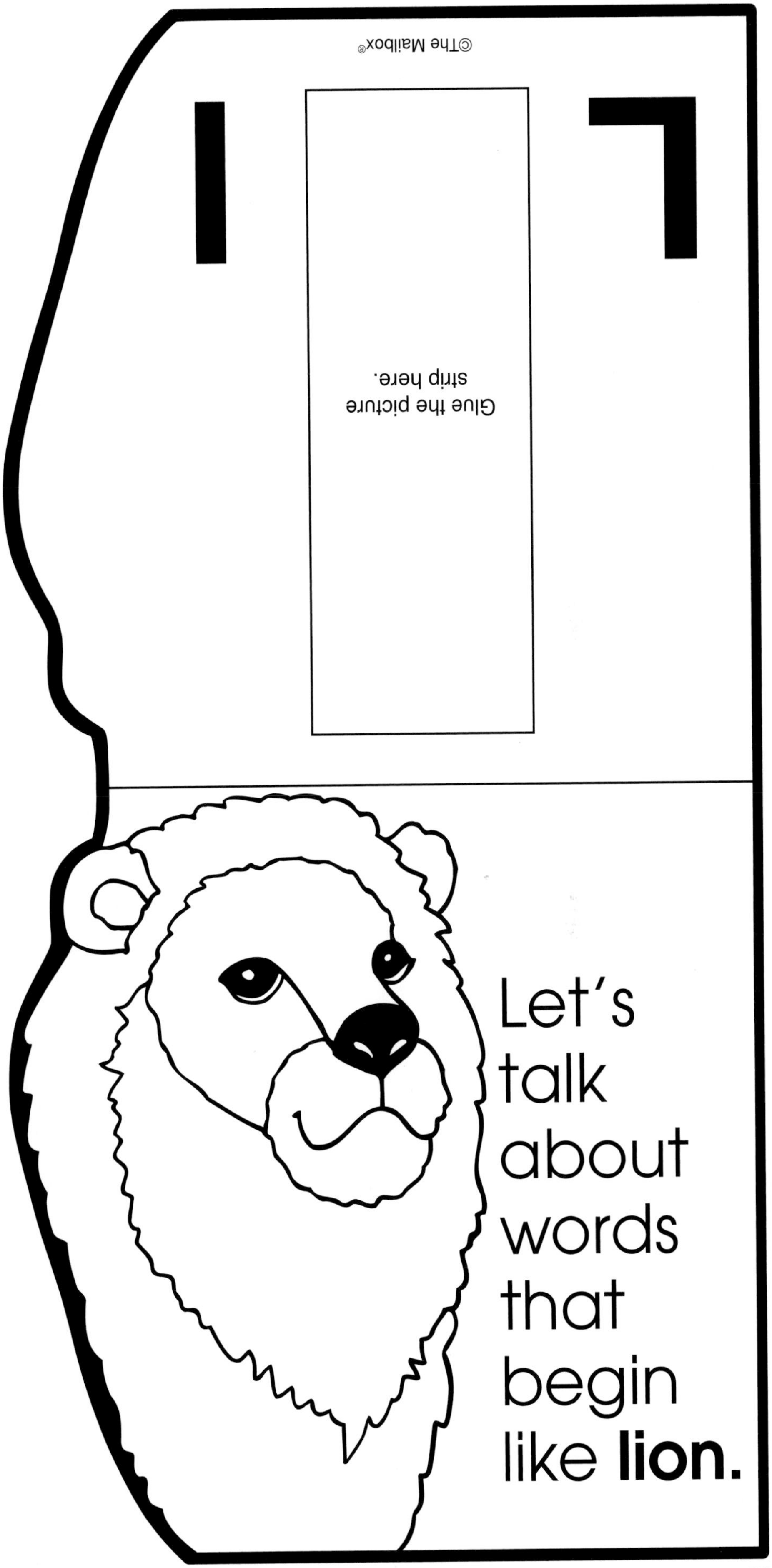
©The Mailbox®
L l
Glue the picture strip here.
Let's talk about words that begin like **lion.**

Using These Cards With "Begins Like Lion" on Page 71

1. Before using pages 70 and 71, photocopy pages 69 and 72 for later use.
2. If desired, laminate the center mat (page 71) and the cards.
3. Cut out the cards.
4. To use, have a child place each picture whose name begins with the /l/ sound on the center mat.
5. Have the child name the pictures on the center mat, listening to confirm that they all begin like *lion.*

These cards may also be used with "Leaping Lions" on page 68.

Begins Like Lion

Name____ /l/ sound

Begins Like Lion

Cut.

Glue.

Sounds Like The Beginning of Mouse

Mouse Melody

If you have a mouse puppet, use it to perform this song the first time. In fact, it could "talk" to your little ones about the sound /m/ in *mouse* and ask them to think of other *m* words to substitute in additional verses. If a mouse is leading the choir, your youngsters will not want to miss a beat.

(sung to the tune of "Bingo")

There is something that starts with /m/.
And do you know its name-o?
/M/, /m/, /m/, /m/, mouse.
/M/, /m/, /m/, /m/, mouse.
/M/, /m/, /m/, /m/, mouse.
Yes! Mousie is its name-o.

Mousie's Messy Nest

Turn your sensory table into a messy mouse nest for this hands-on activity. Put some mittens, masks, small milk cartons, markers, unbreakable mirrors, and empty macaroni boxes in the table. Then cover the items with shredded newspaper to make a mouse's nest and place a toy mouse nearby if you have one. Invite a small group of students to find each item in the nest, say its name, and make the /m/ sound. Once all of the items have been found, ask students to say all the *m* words and replace the items in the nest for the next group to find.

Munch, Little Mouse

Munching like a messy little mouse will tune up listening skills, get out the wiggles, and promote lots of practice with the /m/ sound. Say the lines below with lots of expression, having children chime in on every other line to say each "/M/, /m/, /m/, /m/, /m/" and perform the action mentioned. Afterward, have children recall some words that start with /m/. Write the words on the board and help children discover that they all begin with the letter *m.*

Run to lunch, little mousie!
/M/, /m/, /m/, /m/, /m/. — *Run in place.*
Munch your meal, little mousie.
/M/, /m/, /m/, /m/, /m/. — *Pretend to eat with mouth open.*
Mind your manners, little mousie!
/M/, /m/, /m/, /m/, /m/. — *Pretend to eat with mouth closed.*
What a mess, little mousie!
/M/, /m/, /m/, /m/, /m/. — *Touch cheeks; shake head no.*
Now clean your mess, little mousie!
/M/, /m/, /m/, /m/, /m/. — *Pretend to wash face.*
Was it good, little mousie?
/M/, /m/, /m/, /m/, /m/! — *Rub tummy in circular motion.*

Merry Marching Music

Whether you hum a familiar marching band tune or play a recording of a perky march, your children will get a kick out of incorporating merry music into phonemic practice. Gather the picture cards from page 76 or a selection of small objects, most of which represent a word that begins with *m.* If desired, prepare mouse headbands using the patterns on page 75, and have children wear them and march as mice.

To play, show a picture or object and discuss with your class whether it starts with /m/ like *mouse* does. If it does start with /m/, strike up the band and have children march around in celebration. If it doesn't start with /m/, have the children sit quietly until an *m* word is displayed. Oh, my! Another /m/ word! Let's march!

Making and Using a Mouse Headband

1. Color and cut out the headband and ears.
2. Glue the headband to the center of a 3" x 24" strip of bulletin board paper or a sentence strip.
3. Fit the strip to your head; then staple the ends together.
4. Staple or tape the ears to the sides of the headband.
5. Find someone with whom to discuss the /m/ sound.

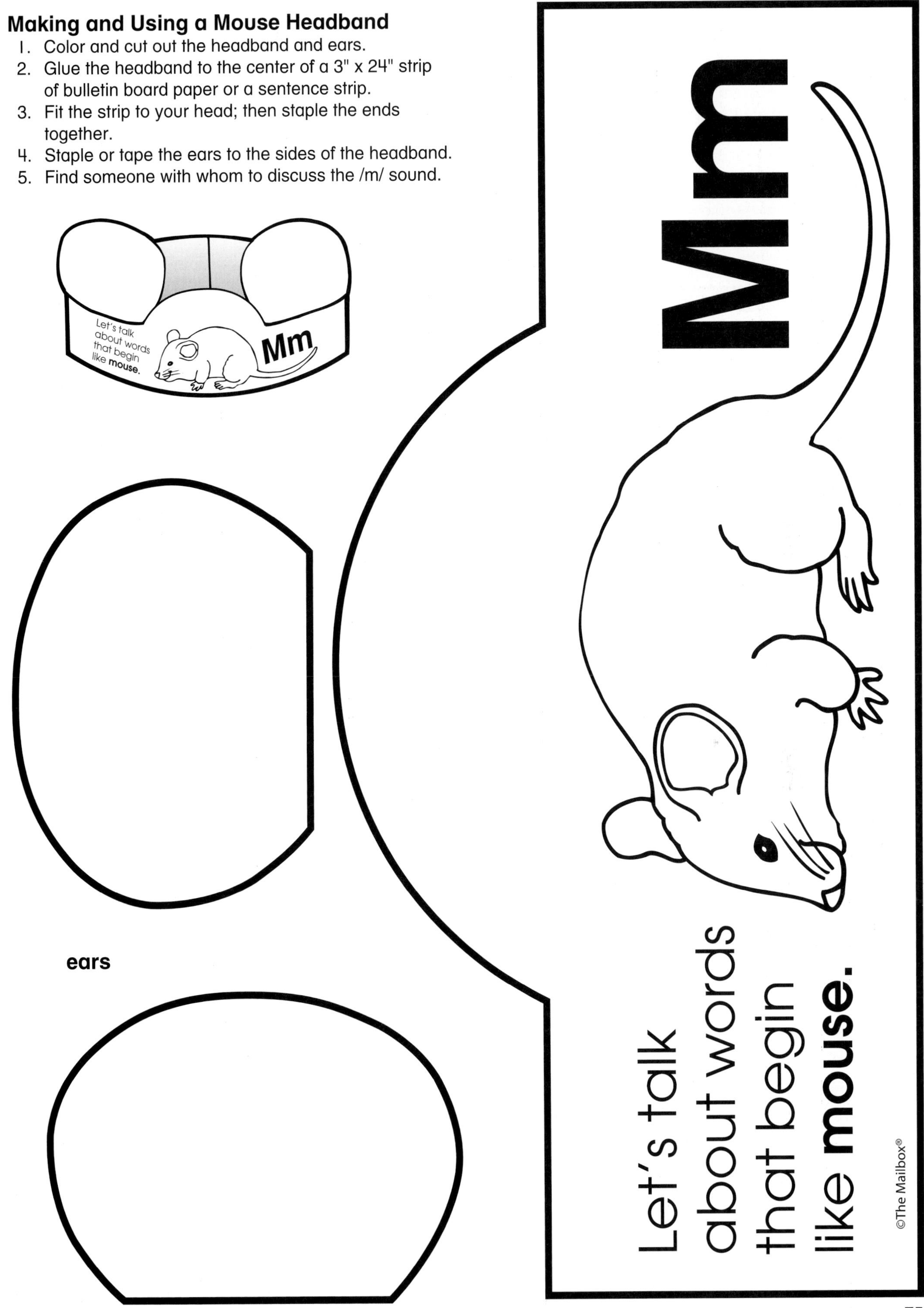

Using These Cards With "Begins Like Mouse" on Page 77

1. Before using pages 76 and 77, photocopy pages 75 and 78 for later use.
2. If desired, laminate the center mat (page 77) and the cards.
3. Cut out the cards.
4. To use, have each child place each picture whose name begins with the /m/ sound on the center mat.
5. Have the child name the pictures on the center mat, listening to confirm that they all begin like *mouse.*

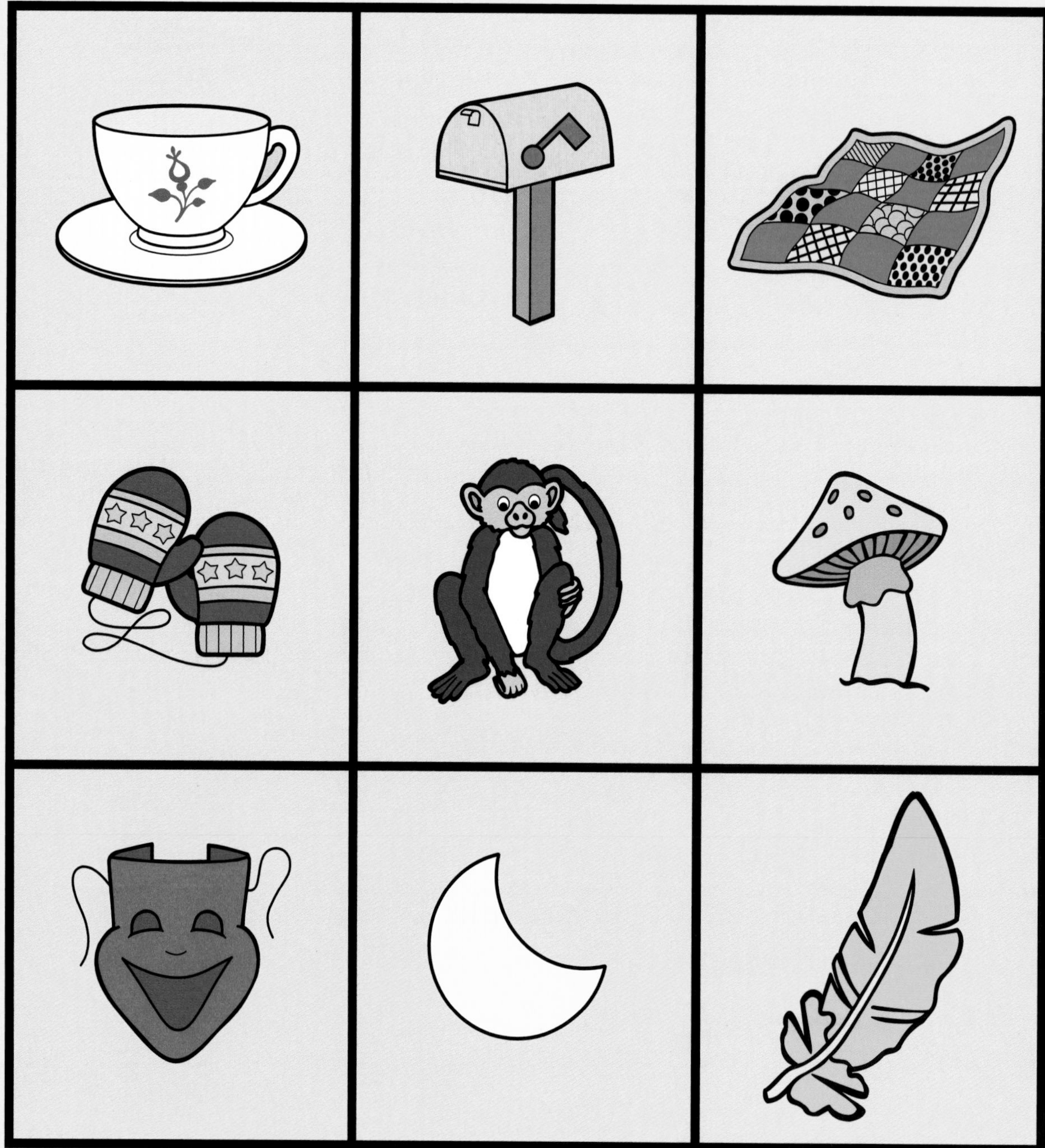

These cards may also be used with "Merry Marching Music" on page 74.

Begins Like Mouse

Name____ /m/ sound

Begins Like Mouse

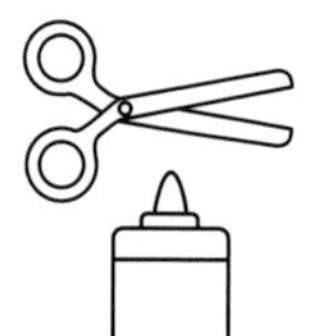

Cut.

Glue.

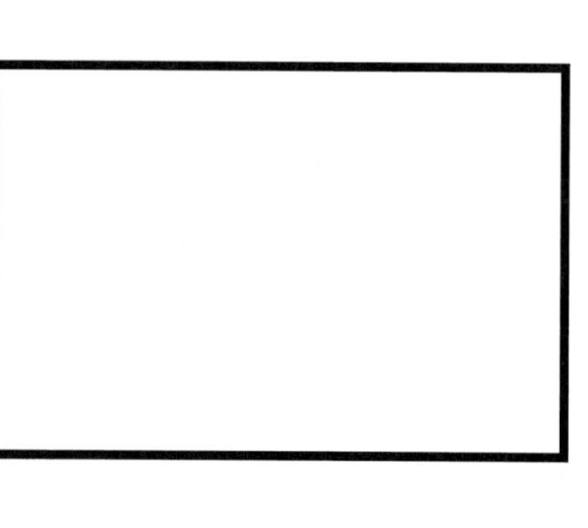

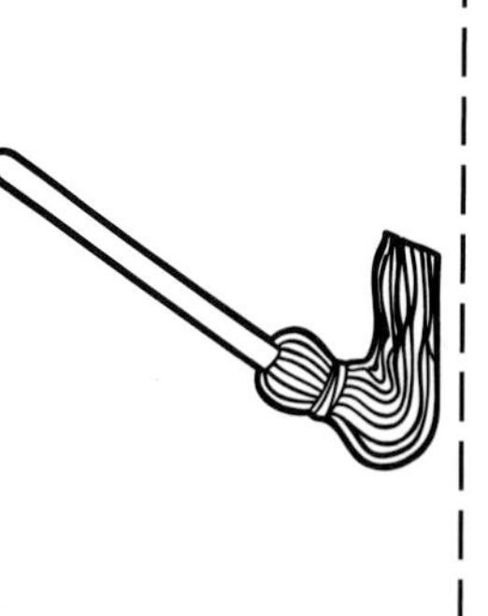

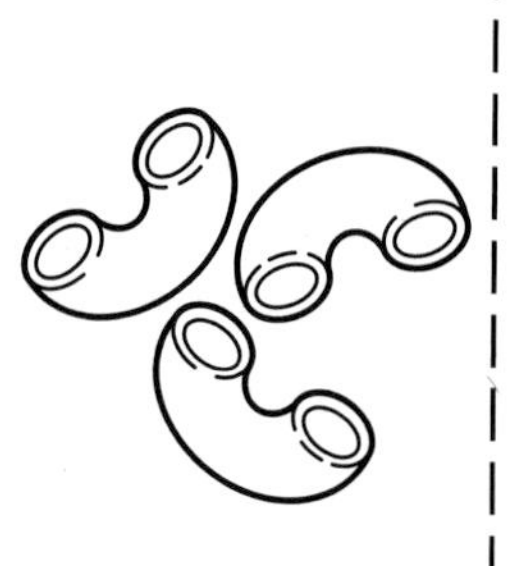

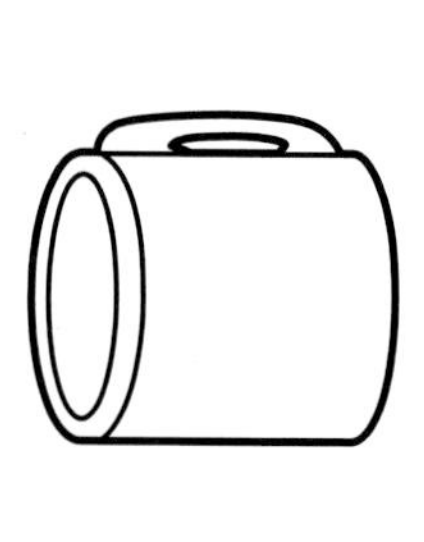

Sounds Like The Beginning of Newt

A Newt Number

Introduce students to the /n/ sound with a new friend, the newt. Display a copy of the newt card on page 81. Explain that newts are small creatures that live part of their lives in water and part on land. Talk about the word *newt* and exaggerate the /n/ sound at the beginning of it. Then sing this song with your children and have them create additional verses by replacing the word *newt* with other words that begin with the /n/ sound.

(sung to the tune of "London Bridge")

Newt begins with /n/, /n/, /n/.
/N/, /n/, /n/. /N/, /n/, /n/.
Newt begins with /n/, /n/, /n/.
Can you hear it?

Nameless No More!

Reinforce the /n/ sound by challenging children to choose a suitable name for a class newt. To prepare, cut out a copy of the newt card on page 81 and glue it to a large craft stick to make a stick puppet. Invite your little ones to sit in a circle. Show them the newt stick puppet and explain that the newt needs a name. Then use the list below to help your youngsters brainstorm names that begin like *newt*. Next, pass the stick puppet around the circle as children sing the song on this page. When the song ends, ask the child who's holding the stick puppet to suggest a name that begins with the /n/ sound. Encourage all the other students to say the suggested name, elongating the beginning sound, if possible, to see whether they agree the name begins like *newt*. Continue playing in this manner until each child has had a turn. Your newt is nameless no more!

Nadia	Nina
Nathan	Natalie
Nick	Ned
Nancy	Noah
Nathaniel	Nate
Nicole	Nicholas
Naomi	Noel
Natasha	

Newt's Challenge

With a new animal friend to their credit and new awareness of the /n/ sound, your children are ready to find other words that begin like the word *newt.* Before teaching the song to your children, survey the room to make sure there are several objects in sight whose names begin with the /n/ sound. Then sing the song, personalizing the verse to send one child scurrying off to find an object whose name begins like *newt.* While she's searching, have her classmates sing another verse.

(sung to the tune of "I'm a Little Teapot")

I'm a little nosy newt
Crawling here and there,
/N/, /n/, /n/, /n/, nosing everywhere.
Can [child's name] find a /n/ word in our room?
We'll stay here. Scurry back soon!

Net Full of Newts

Don't be squeamish. Reach into the net and pull out a newt! You probably won't have to urge children more than once to give this phonemic awareness activity a try. To prepare, place several newt cards (page 81) inside a net produce bag or small fishing net. To play, pass the net to each child in turn. Ask the child holding the net to remove a card, say the word *newt,* and then say a word that begins like *newt.* Have everyone join in as you elongate the /n/ sound while saying the two words. Does everyone agree that they both start with /n/? Great! Pass the net.

Nn

Making and Using a Newt Bracelet

1. Color and cut out the bracelet patterns.
2. Glue the patterns back to back so the pictures show on both sides.
3. Staple the ends together and slip the bracelet on.
4. Find someone with whom to discuss the /n/ sound.

Newt Card

Use with "A Newt Number" and "Nameless No More" on page 79 and "Net Full of Newts" on page 80.

Let's talk about words that begin like **newt.**

Using These Cards With "Begins Like Newt" on Page 83

1. Before using pages 82 and 83, photocopy pages 81 and 84 for later use.
2. If desired, laminate the center mat (page 83) and the cards.
3. Cut out the cards.
4. To use, have a child place each picture whose name begins with the /n/ sound on the center mat.
5. Have the child name the pictures on the center mat, listening to confirm that they all begin like *newt*.

Begins Like Newt

Name____ /n/ sound

Begins Like Newt

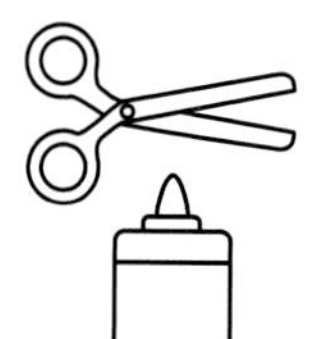

Cut.

Glue.

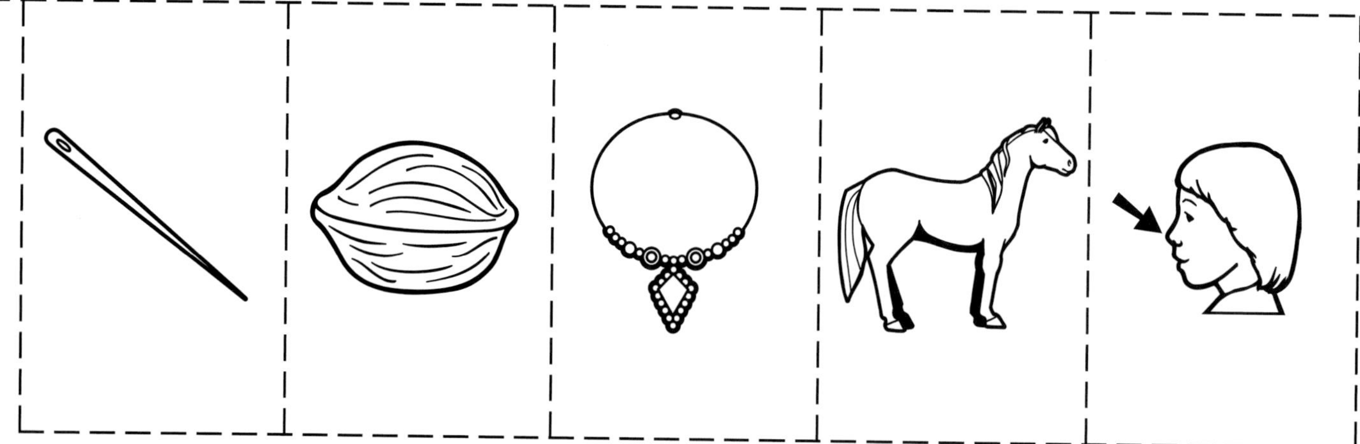

Sounds Like The Beginning of Pig

Piggy Song

Learning the /p/ sound is as easy as pie with this peppy piggy song. Discuss the beginning sound in *pig* before teaching this song to your class.

(sung to the tune of "Twinkle, Twinkle, Little Star")

Listen, listen; lend an ear.
Listen, listen; can you hear?
Pig begins with /p/, you know.
Pig begins with /p/. That's so!
Listen, listen; can you hear?
/P/, /p/, /p/, /p/, loud and clear!

Pet the Pig

If you have a plush pig toy or even if you use an imaginary one, all your children will be anxious to have a turn petting it. To begin the game, seat the children in a circle and give the pig (real or imaginary) to a child. Then say, "Please, please pet the pig!" Invite the child to pet the pig as he answers, "Pet, pet, pet the pig." Next, have him make the /p/ sound as he passes the pig to the next child in the circle. Repeat the game until each child has had a chance to pet the pig.

Puddle of Mud

Could you get enthusiastic about having a mud puddle in your classroom if it improved phonemic awareness? Don't worry. This is a mud puddle even you will love. Put in your sensory table a small toy cooking pot, a pot holder, a small plastic pumpkin, pencils, paper, and other small items that begin with the /p/ sound. Then cover the items with shreds of brown paper bags for an imitation mud puddle. Invite a small group of students to play in the puddle. While there, ask them to find each item, say its name, and make its beginning sound. Once all of the items have been found, ask students to name each of the objects as they place them back in the puddle for the next group to find.

Flippin' Piggy's Pancake

Here's a game your little ones will flip for. To prepare, cut a round pancake shape from craft foam to fit inside a small plastic frying pan. During circle time, begin the game by talking about the /p/ sound at the beginning of *pig, pan,* and *pancake.* Give the pan to one child and have him go to the center of the circle. Prompt the group to chant, "Piggy's pancake's in the pan. Flip it, flip it if you can!" Encourage the child to flip the pancake and catch it in the pan. Next, have the group say, "Please pass Piggy's pancake." Then have the child make the /p/ sound as he passes the pan to a child who was seated next to him in the circle. Continue in this manner until each child has had a turn.

Making and Using a Pig Necklace

1. Color the pig.
2. Cut out the pendant and the picture strip along the bold outer lines.
3. Staple the ends of a ¾" x 26" crepe paper streamer strip to make a necklace.
4. Fold the pendant in half, slip the streamer strip inside, and glue the folded paper closed.
5. Name the pictures on the picture strip, listening for the /p/ sound at the beginning of each word. Glue the picture strip to the back of the pendant.
6. Find someone with whom to discuss the /p/ sound.

Using These Cards with "Begins Like Pig" on Page 89

1. Before using pages 88 and 89, photocopy pages 87 and 90 for later use.
2. If desired, laminate the center mat (page 89) and the cards.
3. Cut out the cards.
4. To use, have a child place each picture whose name begins with the /p/ sound on the center mat.
5. Have the child name the pictures on the center mat, listening to confirm that they all begin like *pig*.

Begins Like Pig

Name____ /p/ sound

Begins Like Pig

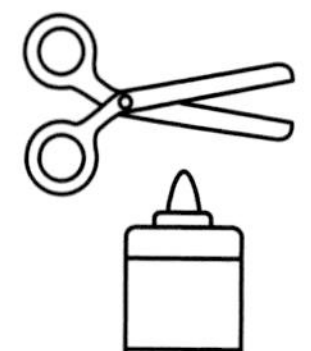

Cut.

Glue.

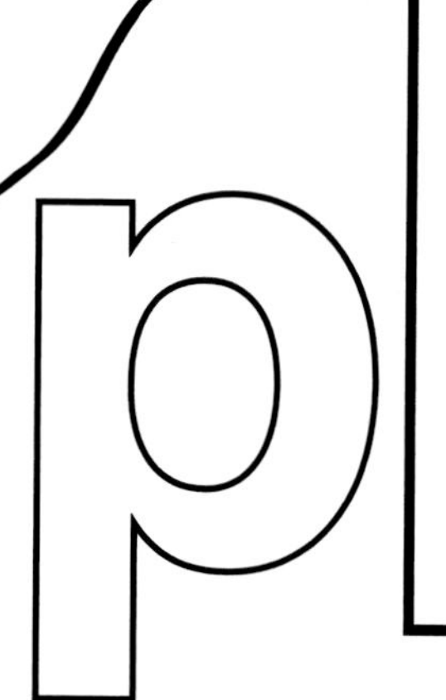

Sounds Like The Beginning of Quail

Q and *Qu*

Most *q* words, like *quail,* begin with *qu*. The letter *q* makes the /k/ sound, and the letter *u* following it makes the /w/ sound. In this section, we've indicated the *q* sound as /k/. If you want your children to focus on the *qu* blend instead, you can easily adapt the ideas by focusing on the blend's sound, /kw/.

The Quail Song

With this simple song, students will learn *q*'s /k/ sound as quick as a wink! Later, when children are ready to expand their range of *q* words, modify the verse to fit other *q* words such as *queen* and *quarter*.

(sung to the tune of "The Wheels on the Bus")

Quail is a critter that starts with /k/.
/K/, /k/, /k/. /K/, /k/, /k/.
Quail is a critter that starts with /k/.
Say it with me.

Quick, Quail, Quick!

Your little ones will be quick to pick up on the /k/ sound of *q* when they play this variation of Duck, Duck, Goose. Have students sit in a circle, and give a child a copy of the quail card on page 93. Discuss the word *quail* and its beginning sound. Then, as the child with the card walks around the outside of the circle tapping classmates' heads, direct her to say the /k/ sound each time. Have the child say, "Quail!" when she taps the head of the child who will stand up and chase her around the circle. Children seated in the circle will have to keep their listening ears on to catch up with this quick quail!

Quiet All Around

Give children the opportunity to focus on the beginning sound of *quail* and *quiet* in this hushed song. Once your little ones have learned the verse, have half your students sing it to the other half so that the listeners can focus on the similarities of the beginning sounds in *quail* and *quiet.*

(sung to the tune of "Twinkle, Twinkle, Little Star")

Quail, quail, not a sound.
Quiet, quiet all around.
Not a whisper, not a peep.
Everyone is fast asleep.
Quail, quail, not a sound.
Quiet, quiet all around.

Little Quail Action Poem

Introduce this action poem to your children. Then talk about all the words in it that begin like *quail.*

Little quail, little quail, proud as a queen,	*Smile, stick out chest, and look proud.*
Quietest bird we've ever seen,	*Flap arms softly and tiptoe in place.*
Quivers and quavers getting ready to fly,	*Tremble and flap arms.*
Then flaps off quickly through the sky.	*Flap arms quickly and run in place.*

Making and Using a Quail Bracelet

1. Color and cut out the bracelet patterns.
2. Glue the patterns back to back so the pictures show on both sides.
3. Staple the ends together and slip the bracelet on.
4. Find someone with whom to discuss the sound at the beginning of *quail* (/k/).

Quail Card

Use with "Quick, Quail, Quick!" on page 91.

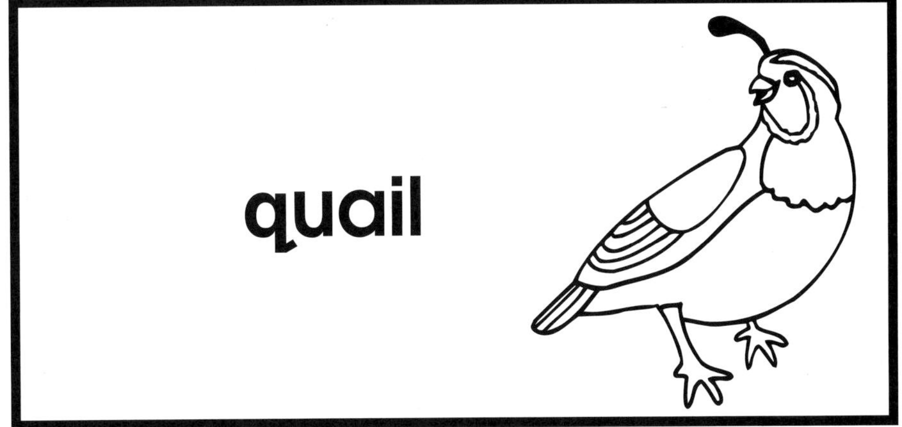

Qq

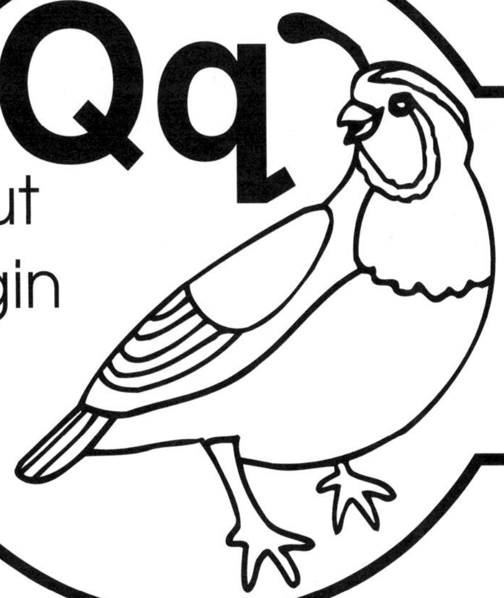

Let's talk about words that begin like **quail.**

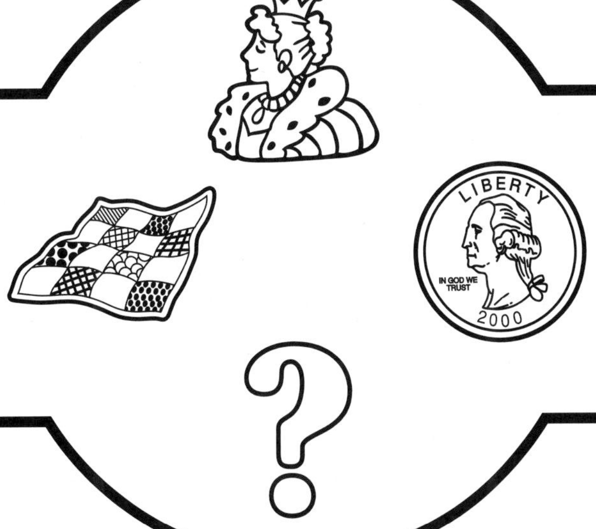

LIBERTY

IN GOD WE TRUST

2000

?

Using These Cards With "Begins Like Quail" on Page 95

1. Before using pages 94 and 95, photocopy pages 93 and 96 for later use.
2. If desired, laminate the center mat (page 95) and the cards.
3. Cut out the cards.
4. To use, have a child place each picture whose name begins like *quail* on the center mat.
5. Have the child name the picture words on the center mat, listening to confirm that they all begin like *quail.*

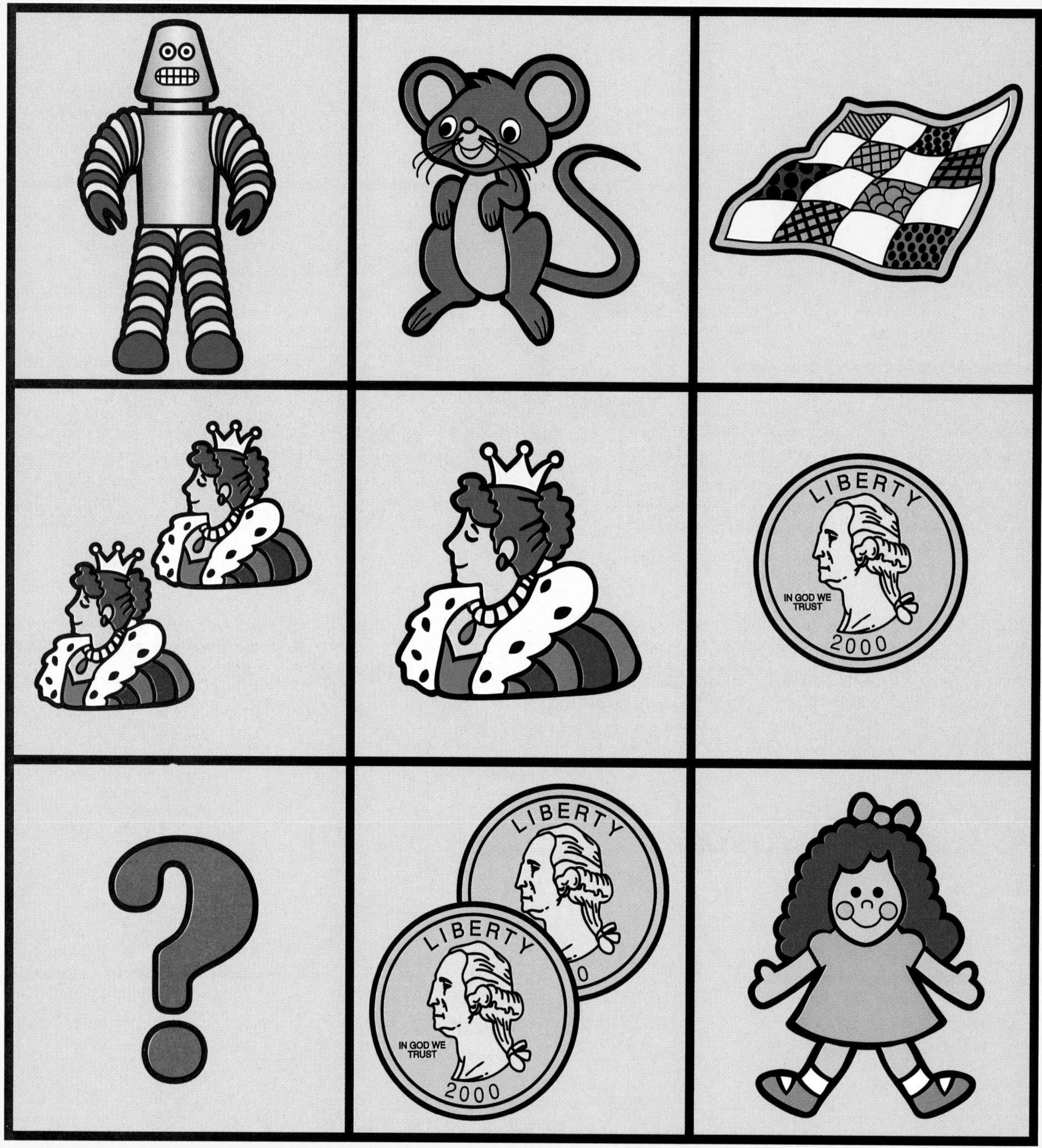

Begins Like Quail

Name____ /q/ sound

Begins Like Quail

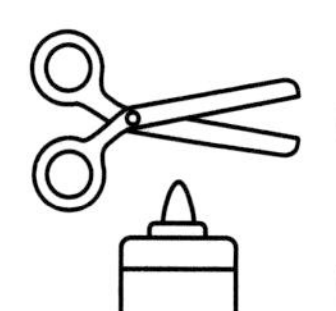

Cut.

Glue.

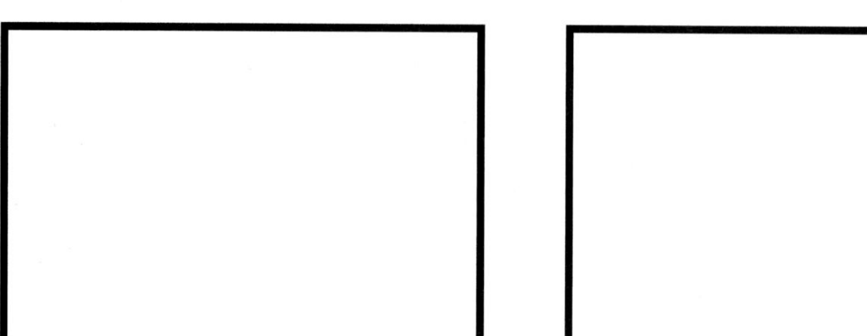

Sounds Like The Beginning of Raccoon

The Raccoon Song

Ready to teach the /r/ sound? Try this tune!

(sung to the tune of "Go in and out the Window")

Oh, say *raccoon* and listen.
Oh, say *raccoon* and listen.
Oh, say *raccoon* and listen.
Raccoon begins with /r/.

Raccoon's Rectangle

In this group activity, everyone gets into the action. To prepare, use masking tape to create a large rectangular area. To remind the children that *rectangle* and *raccoon* both start with the /r/ sound, use clear Con-Tact covering to adhere a large drawing of a raccoon along the rectangle's perimeter. Gather a toy rake, a ruler, a rattle, several pieces of ribbon, a short length of rope, an artificial rose, a plush rabbit toy, and a few items whose names don't begin with /r/. Place them in a basket or bucket near the rectangle.

To play, ask students to help you choose some things whose names start like *raccoon* to put inside Raccoon's rectangle. Hold up each item, in turn, and say its name. If students think the item's name begins with the /r/ sound, prompt them to respond by saying, "Put the [/r/ word] inside Raccoon's rectangle." If the item's name does not begin with /r/, have them set it aside. After all the items have been sorted, encourage children to visit this area during center time to repeat the activity with a partner.

Rr

Raccoon Action Poem

Running a race will rev up your students' enthusiasm and promote lots of practice listening for the /r/ sound. If your students make headbands (page 99), have them sport them during this activity. Say the lines below with lots of expression, asking children to perform each action described. Afterward, have children recall some words that start with /r/ like *raccoon* does.

Come on, Raccoon, run in place.	*Run very slowly in place.*
Are you ready for the race?	*Run in place at a moderate pace.*
Raccoon, run and ramble along.	*Run quickly in place.*
Run, run, run. The race is long!	*Run more slowly in place. Pant as if very tired.*
Run, run, run! Pick up the pace!	*Run quickly in place.*
Now rejoice! You've won the race!	*Smile and make the victory sign with fingers.*

Rummaging Around for /R/

Explain to your little ones that in this activity you'll all be rummaging around like raccoons sometimes do, but instead of searching for tasty tidbits, you'll be searching for items whose names begin like *raccoon.* Suit up by having your students wear their headbands (page 99), if desired. As you stroll around your classroom or school, sing the song below, stopping frequently to name some of the items you see and to celebrate when an item whose name begins with the /r/ sound is discovered.

(sung to the tune of "I've Been Working on the Railroad"—the third verse: "Someone's in the kitchen with Dinah...")

We're going to find some /r/ things
In this place we know, oh, oh, oh.
We're going to find some /r/ things
Our big ears will tell us so.

Rr

Making and Using a Raccoon Headband

1. Color and cut out the headband pattern and ears.
2. Glue the headband pattern to the center of a 3" x 24" strip of bulletin board paper or a sentence strip.
3. Fit the strip to your head; then staple the ends together.
4. Tape the ears to the sides of the headband.
5. Find someone with whom to discuss the /r/ sound.

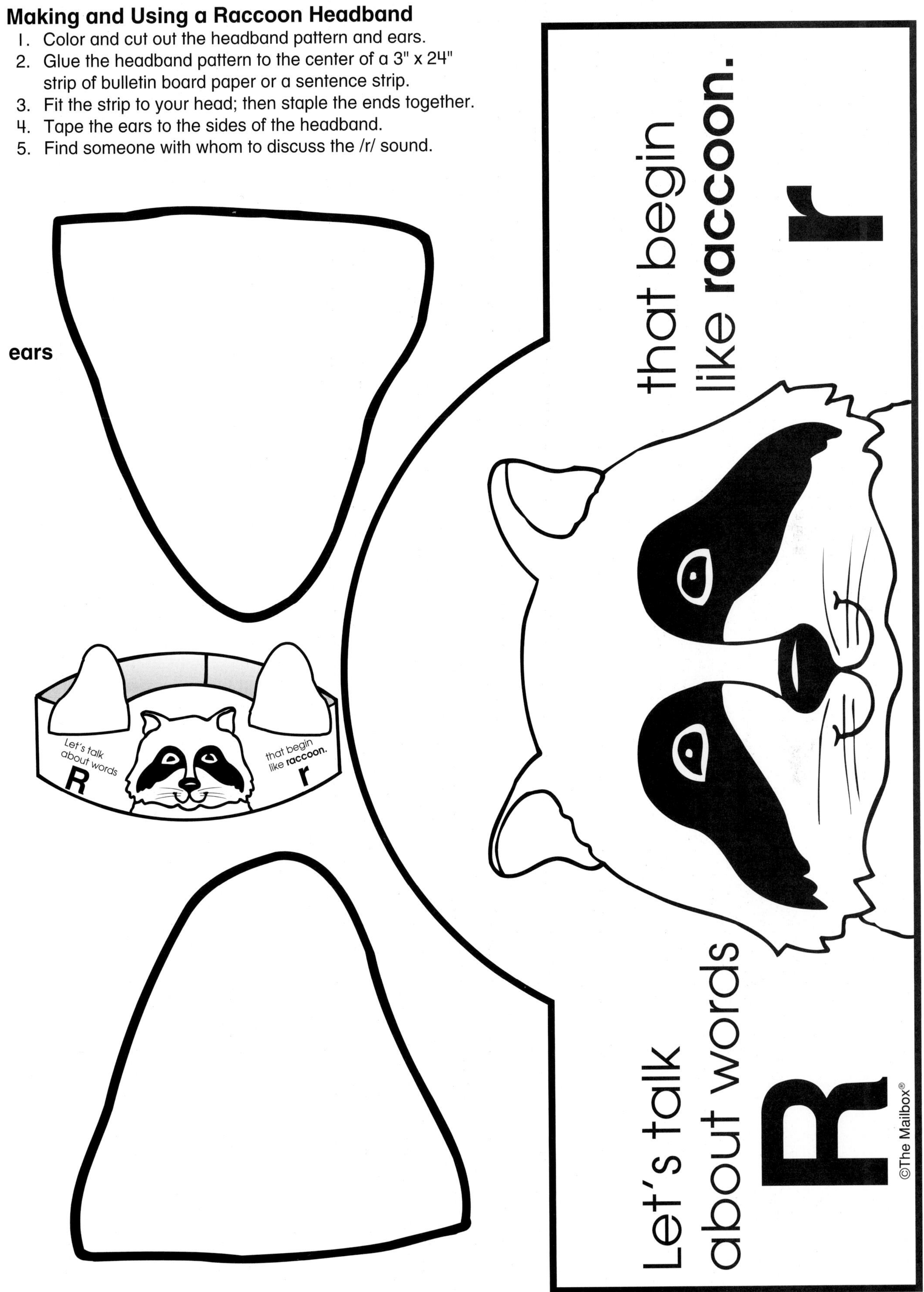

Using These Cards With "Begins Like Raccoon" on Page 101

1. Before using pages 100 and 101, photocopy pages 99 and 102 for later use.
2. If desired, laminate the center mat (page 101) and the cards.
3. Cut out the cards.
4. To use, have a child place each picture whose name begins with the /r/ sound on the center mat.
5. Have the child name the pictures on the center mat, listening to confirm that they all begin like *raccoon.*

Begins Like Raccoon

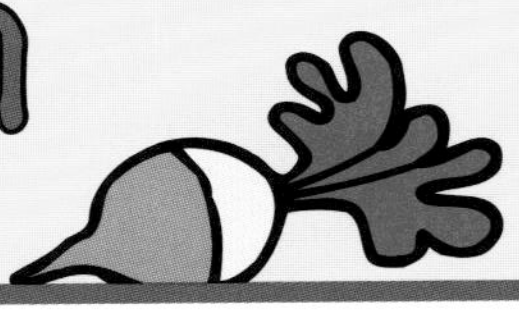

Name____ /r/ sound

Begins Like Raccoon

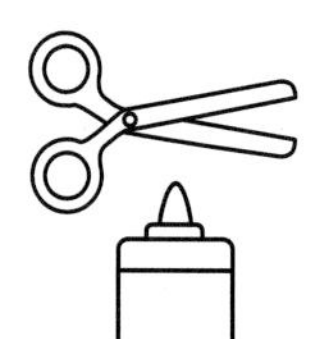

Cut.

Glue.

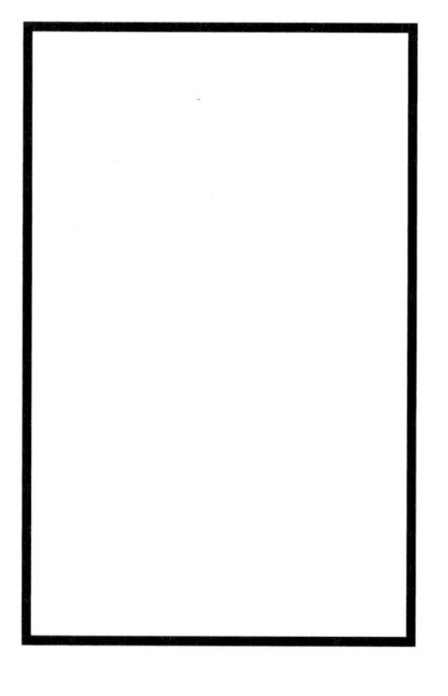

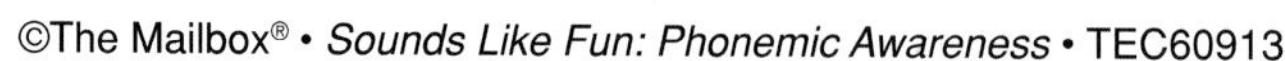

Sounds Like The Beginning of Seal

Seal Serenade

Learning the /s/ sound is simple for students when they sing this song. Introduce the sound by showing students a seal toy or picture and discussing the first sound in the word *seal.* Then sing the song below. After singing it a few times, ask your children to think of another word that begins like *seal.* When everyone agrees that it does, swim on into another verse, this time substituting that word for *seal.*

(sung to the tune of "Short'nin' Bread")

Seal begins with /s/. Oh, can you hear it?
Seal begins with /s/, /s/, /s/, /s/, /s/.
/S/—what a swell sound. Say it with me.
/S/—what a swell sound. Yes sirree!

Seal's Swimming Pool

Make a splash with youngsters by turning your sensory table into a swimming pool for a seal. Place a toy saw, a die-cut sun shape, several socks, and some numeral 6 and 7 cutouts in the table. Then cover the items with shredded blue paper to create an imitation swimming pool. Invite a small group of students to explore the swimming pool, find each item, say its name, and listen for the /s/ sound. Once all of the items have been found, ask students to hide them in the pool again for the next group to find.

Seal's Surprise

Seal has some special sentences in store for your youngsters. Challenge children to think of a word that begins like *seal* to complete each sentence. Celebrate each success by singing "Seal Serenade" (page 103).

A seal lives in the _____. *(sea)*

The water in the sea tastes _____. *(salty)*

A bird sometimes seen at the beach is a _____. *(seagull)*

Two seals that look exactly alike are the _____. *(same)*

A seal's skin is not hard; it's _____. *(soft)*

When a seal barks, it makes a _____. *(sound)*

Six Words That Begin Like *Seal*

Put six children's socks (the brighter the better) in a brown paper sack to play this circle-time game. If desired, you may also prepare for this activity by having children make a collage of magazine pictures that begin like the word *seal* and post it near your circle-time area. To play, pass the sack to each child in turn. Prompt the child to remove one sock at a time from the sack. As she removes each one, help her say a word that begins like *seal.* (Explain that *sock, sack*, and *seal* can be her first three words with the /s/ sound.) What a super way to extend children's knowledge of /s/ words!

Ss

Making and Using a Seal Necklace

1. Color the seal.
2. Cut out the pendant and the picture strip along the bold outer lines.
3. Staple the ends of a ¾" x 26" crepe paper streamer strip to make a necklace.
4. Fold the pendant in half, slip the streamer strip inside, and glue the folded paper closed.
5. Name the pictures on the picture strip, listening for the /s/ sound at the beginning of each word. Glue the picture strip to the back of the pendant.
6. Find someone with whom to discuss the /s/ sound.

Note: Some words that have the same beginning sound as *seal* begin with *s,* and some begin with *c.* The focus of this activity is on *s* words with the same beginning sound as in *seal.* But *c* words, such as *circus,* may also be mentioned since they share the beginning sound of *seal.*

/s/ picture strip

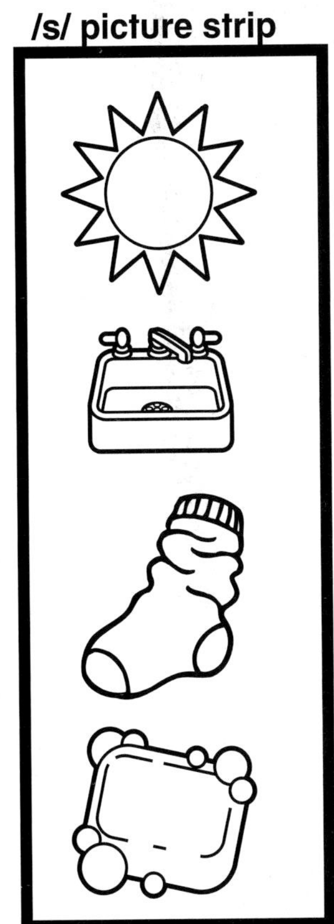

Glue the picture strip here.

s S

Let's talk about words that begin like **seal.**

Ss

Using These Cards With "Begins Like Seal" on Page 107

1. Before using pages 106 and 107, photocopy pages 105 and 108 for later use.
2. If desired, laminate the center mat (page 107) and the cards.
3. Cut out the cards.
4. To use, have a child place each picture that begins with the /s/ sound on the center mat.
5. Have the child name the pictures on the center mat, listening to confirm that they all begin like *seal.*

Begins Like Seal

Name____ /s/ sound

Begins Like Seal

Cut.

Glue.

Sounds Like The Beginning of Turtle

Turtle Tune

This terrific little tune can make learning the /t/ sound a whole lot of fun! Locate a turtle puppet or make a turtle stick puppet from a simple illustration. Then let the beginning-sound fun commence. Introduce the turtle puppet to your students and have them listen carefully as you say, "Turtle," emphasizing its first letter. Tune up your vocal chords. Here we go!

(sung to the tune of "Camptown Races")

Turtle, turtle starts with /t/. Listen. Listen.
Turtle, turtle starts with /t/. Say it now with me.
/T/, /t/! Say it loud. /T/, /t/! Say it strong.
Turtle, turtle starts with /t/. Let's sing it all day long.

Turtle Says

This variation of Simon Says will make your little ones cautious about getting tricked. Gather together easy-to-find items whose names begin with the /t/ sound, such as a tissue tube, a roll of tape, a man's tie, a toy truck, a towel, a plastic turtle, and a toy telephone. Include a couple of other objects whose names don't begin with the /t/ sound. To play, explain to your students that Turtle Says is a listening game. Say, "Turtle says to touch your toes if the word you hear starts with the /t/ sound." From your collection of items, hold up and name one object. Watch to see whether listeners touch their toes or not. Talk about the beginning sound of each word. Continue until each item has been discussed. Watch out! This game can be tricky.

Tired Turtle

Telling this sleepy action tale is a good way to reinforce the /t/ sound. After reading it to and acting it out with your children, ask them to recall words from the story that start like *turtle.*

Turtle is too, too tired today.	*Yawn.*
But Turtle didn't run, and Turtle didn't play.	*Shake head no.*
Turtle is too, too tired to talk	*Slump over as if very tired.*
Just because he took his turtle walk!	*Walk very slowly in place.*
Turtle is /t/, /t/ tired today.	*Yawn.*
But Turtle didn't run, and Turtle didn't play.	*Shake head no.*
Turtle is /t/, /t/ tired to talk.	*Slump over as if very tired.*
Blame it on his /t/, /t/ turtle walk!	*Walk very slowly in place and yawn.*

They Are All Around

Now that your children are familiar with the /t/ sound, they may be able to find words that start with /t/ all around them. Give each child a turtle card from page 111 and remind the class of the beginning sound of *turtle.* Sing the first verse of the song shown as children move around the room looking for other things whose names start with /t/. Provide assistance as necessary. As the song ends, have everyone sit in a circle. Ask volunteers to name the objects they saw whose names begin with /t/. To celebrate each child's success, personalize the second verse and include the /t/ word that was located. Then hop up and start the whole thing over again.

(sung to the tune of "For He's a Jolly Good Fellow")

Let's go in search of /t/ words.
Let's go in search of /t/ words.
Let's go in search of /t/ words.
And then we will sit down.

[Child's name] found a /t/ word.
[Child's name] found a /t/ word.
[Child's name] found a /t/ word.
[Object name] begins with /t/!

Use with "They Are All Around" on page 110.

Making and Using a Turtle Bracelet

1. Color and cut out the bracelet patterns.
2. Glue the patterns back to back so the pictures show on both sides.
3. Staple the ends together and slip the bracelet on.
4. Find someone with whom to discuss the /t/ sound.

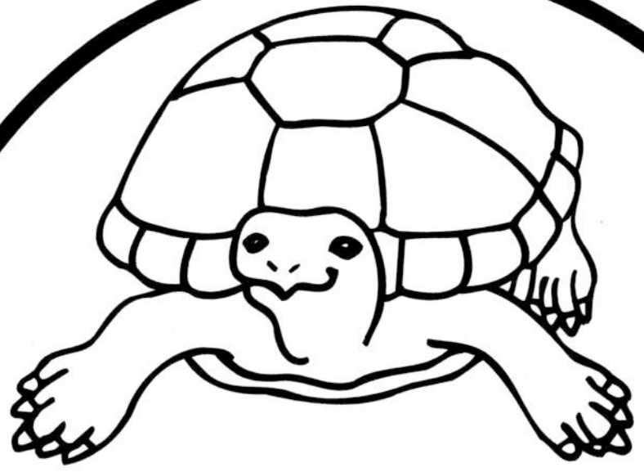

Let's talk about words that begin like **turtle.**

Tt

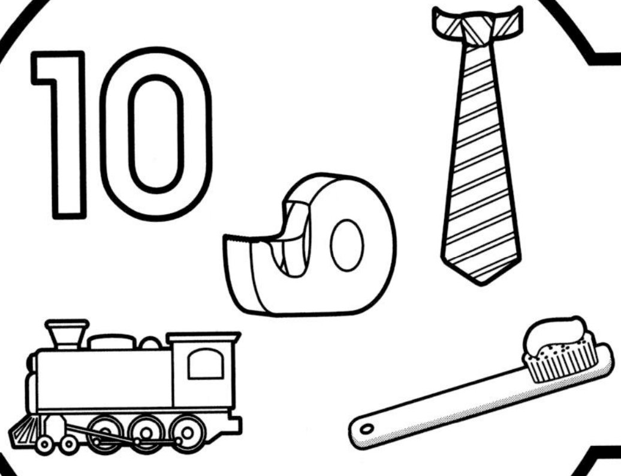

10

Using These Cards With "Begins Like Turtle" on Page 113

1. Before using pages 112 and 113, photocopy pages 111 and 114 for later use.
2. If desired, laminate the center mat (page 113) and the cards.
3. Cut out the cards.
4. To use, have a child place each picture whose name begins with the /t/ sound on the center mat.
5. Have each child name the pictures on the center mat, listening to confirm that they all begin like *turtle.*

Begins Like Turtle

Name____ /t/ sound

Begins Like Turtle

Cut.

Glue.

t

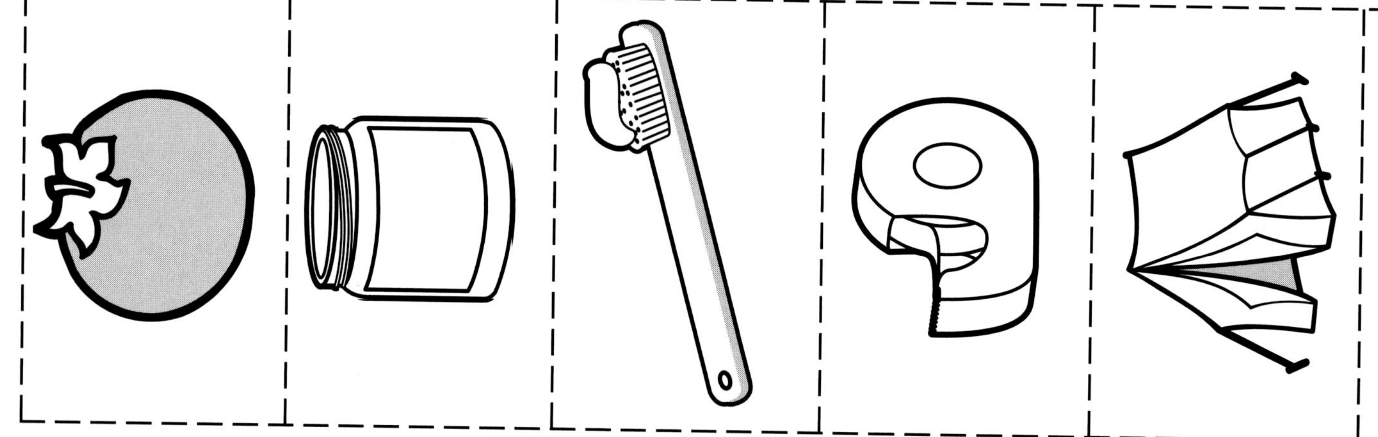

Sounds Like The Beginning of Vulture

The Vulture Song

This easy song makes a nice introduction to the /v/ sound. First, show children a picture of a vulture and find out whether anyone has seen one or knows something about vultures. After singing this song a couple of times, ask your children to think of something else whose name begins like *vulture.* When you've agreed that it does, start into another verse.

(sung to the tune of "Twinkle, Twinkle, Little Star")

/V/, /v/, vultures far and near.
Listen carefully, my dear.
/V/, /v/, /v/. It sounds just so.
/V/, /v/, /v/, /v/. Now we know.
/V/, /v/, vultures flying round.
Can you hear the /v/, /v/ sound?

Vote for Vulture's Words

Put some verve into learning the /v/ sound with this group activity. To prepare, cut a wide slot in the lid of a plain shoebox to convert it into a ballot box. Gather the picture cards from page 118. Then display the cards and the box on a table. To begin, show students the box and tell them that it is Vulture's voting box. Talk about what voting is, and guide students to notice that *vulture* and *vote* both start with the /v/ sound. Explain that Vulture wants them to vote only for things whose names begin with /v/. Next, hold up each picture card in turn and say its name. If the item's name begins with the /v/ sound, have a child drop it into the box. When all the pictures have been considered, open the box and name the words in unison with your students, encouraging them to listen to confirm that the beginning sounds are all the same. Later, place the box and the picture cards in a center for independent use.

Vulture's Valentines

Reinforce the /v/ sound with this small-group Concentration game. To prepare, make two copies of the cards on page 118. Cut out the cards and set aside those whose names do not begin with the /v/ sound. Glue each of the remaining cards to one of twelve identical construction paper hearts.

Just before playing the game, discuss the beginning sound of *valentines* with a small group of children and explain that this game involves more words that start with the /v/ sound. Place the cards facedown on a tabletop in several rows. Then have children take turns flipping two cards in search of a matching pair. When a child locates a pair, have him identify the pictures' beginning sound and verify that it starts like *valentine.* Have him hold those cards as play continues. When all the matches have been found, have children name all the /v/ pictures while listening for the /v/ sound.

A Vulture's-Eye View

Say this poem with lots of expression, and soon your children will imagine themselves soaring overhead like vultures. Before you take flight, encourage children to listen for other words in the poem that begin with the /v/ sound. Settle back down to earth by talking about words in the poem that begin like *vulture.*

Vulture lives out in the valley.	*Extend arm forward and point.*
His land is very wide.	*Stretch arms out wide.*
He flies up high	*Extend arm straight up and point.*
For a vulture's-eye view	*Point to eye.*
Of his very vast countryside.	*Stretch arms out wide.*
Vulture flies over his valley,	*Flap arms.*
High up in the skies.	*Flap arms and look up.*
He views villages,	*Flap arms and look down.*
One, two, three,	*Hold up three fingers, one at a time.*
With his very sharp vulture eyes.	*Point to both eyes, wink, and nod affirmingly.*

Making and Using a Vulture Necklace

1. Color the vulture.
2. Cut out the pendant and the picture strip along the bold outer lines.
3. Staple the ends of a ¾" x 26" crepe paper streamer strip to make a necklace.
4. Fold the pendant in half, slip the streamer strip inside, and glue the folded paper closed.
5. Name the pictures on the picture strip, listening for the /v/ sound at the beginning of each word. Glue the picture strip to the back of the pendant.
6. Find someone with whom to discuss the /v/ sound.

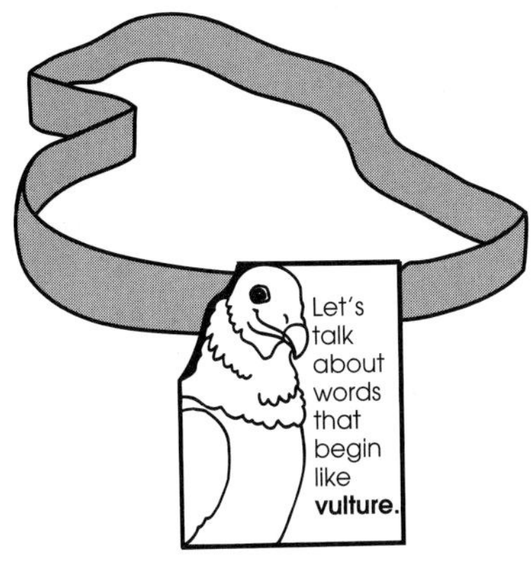

Let's talk about words that begin like vulture.

/v/ picture strip

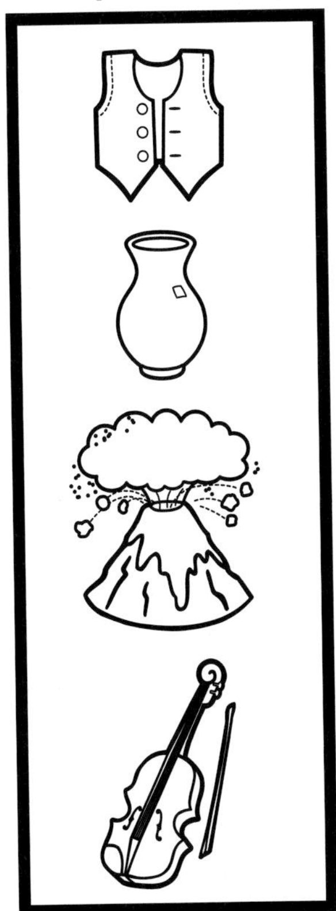

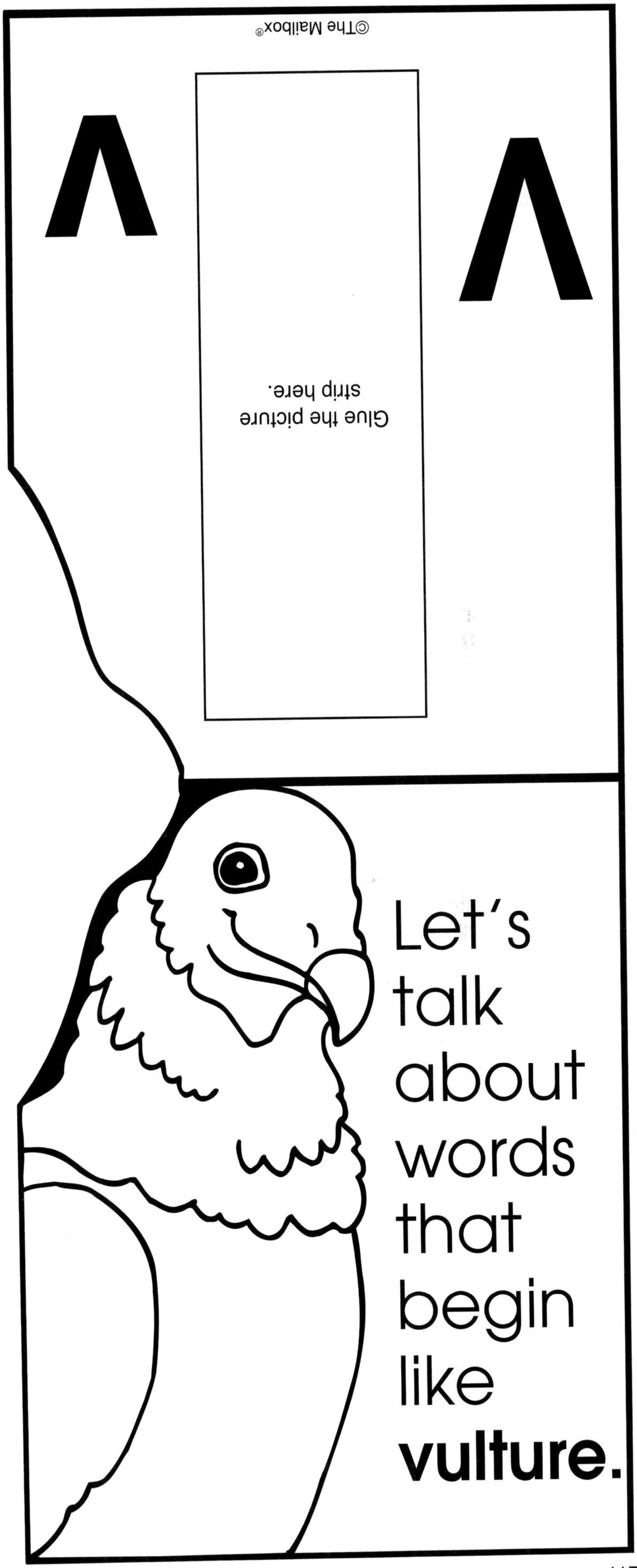
©The Mailbox®
V
V
Glue the picture strip here.
Let's talk about words that begin like vulture.

Using These Cards With "Begins Like Vulture" on Page 119

1. Before using pages 118 and 119, photocopy pages 117 and 120 for later use.
2. If desired, laminate the center mat (page 119) and the cards.
3. Cut out the cards.
4. To use, have a child place each picture whose name begins with the /v/ sound on the center mat.
5. Have the child name the pictures on the center mat, listening to confirm that they all begin like *vulture.*

These cards may also be used with "Vote for Vulture's Words" on page 115 and "Vulture's Valentines" on page 116.

Begins Like Vulture

Name________________________________ /v/ sound

Begins Like Vulture

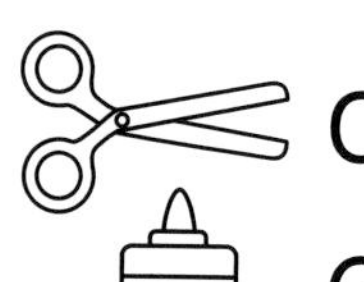
Cut.
Glue.

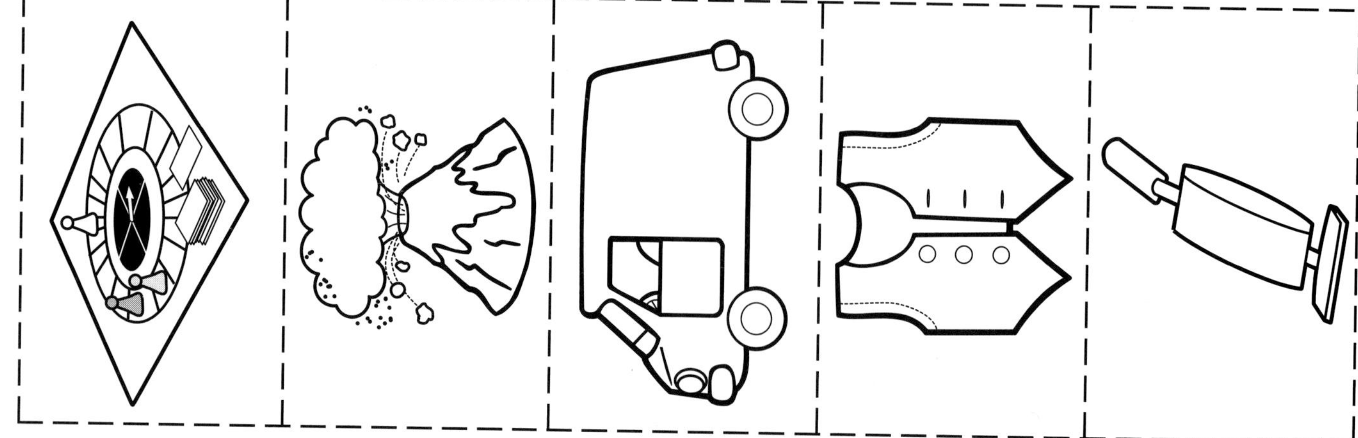

Sounds Like The Beginning of Wolf

Wolf Song

Win over little learners with this simple song about the /w/ sound. To introduce the sound, show the wolf miniposter from page 15 and talk with children about the sound they hear at the beginning of the word *wolf.* Then teach children the song below and march around together singing it. Afterward, have children think of other words that begin with the /w/ sound and substitute each of those words for *wolf* in the verse.

(sung to the tune of "The Farmer in the Dell")

Oh, *wolf* begins with /w/.
Oh, *wolf* begins with /w/.
Let's use our ears to hear, my dears,
That *wolf* begins with /w/.

Tracking 'em Down

Hunting for words that begin like *wolf* will be a fun pursuit in this simple center. To prepare, cover a tabletop with bulletin board paper. Glue pictures to it, many of which begin with the /w/ sound. Place the pictures far enough apart that there is a perimeter of blank space around each one. Also place on the table a pawprint stamp, an ink pad, and a plush wolf if available. Explain to students that when they visit the center, they are to "track down" things with names that begin like *wolf.* Have each child stamp a pawprint by each picture that begins with the /w/ sound. When everyone has visited the center, talk to students about the words that are surrounded by pawprints. Say the words in a series to see whether childen can hear a /w/ sound at the beginning of each.

On the Prowl

In this game, children go on the prowl for objects whose names begin like *wolf.* In advance, put together a collection of items that represent words that start with the /w/ sound. Include things like a wagon, water bottle, watch, worm, and wallet. Add a couple of things to your collection whose names don't begin with the /w/ sound. To play the game, first remind children about the beginning sound of *wolf.* Then explain that in this game, Wolfie wants them to find objects whose names begin just like *wolf.* Select a child to be first, perhaps a child whose name begins with /w/. Have the other children sing the song with you while she picks an object that starts with the /w/ sound. At the end of the song, have the group decide whether the object's name starts just like *wolf.* Provide assistance as necessary. Repeat until each child has had a turn.

(sung to the tune of "Did You Ever See a Lassie?")

Can you quickly find a /w/ word, a /w/ word, a /w/ word?
Can you quickly find a /w/ word and put it right here?
/W/, /w/, /w/, /w/, /w/, /w/. /W/, /w/, /w/, /w/, /w/, /w/.
Wolfie hopes you find a /w/ word and put it right here.

Waddle, Wiggle, Wobble

This infectious action song features verbs that start with the /w/ sound. If your class walks and waddles and wiggles and wobbles through the hallway singing it, you'll probably start a new trend. Just remember to tell the folks you pass that your children are learning the beginning sound of *walk, waddle, wiggle,* and *wobble.*

(sung to the tune of "Shortnin' Bread")

Wolfie's favorite way to move is walk, walk, walk, walk. *Step in place, moving arms.*
Wolfie's favorite way to move is walk on down. *Step in place, moving arms.*

Ducky's favorite way to move is waddle, waddle. *Rock from side to side.*
Ducky's favorite way to move is waddle on down. *Rock from side to side.*

Wormie's favorite way to move is wiggle, wiggle. *Wiggle body with arms over head.*
Wormie's favorite way to move is wiggle on down. *Wiggle body with arms over head.*

Baby's favorite way to move is wobble, wobble. *Teeter around, arms stiff at sides.*
Baby's favorite way to move is wobble on down. *Teeter around, arms stiff at sides.*

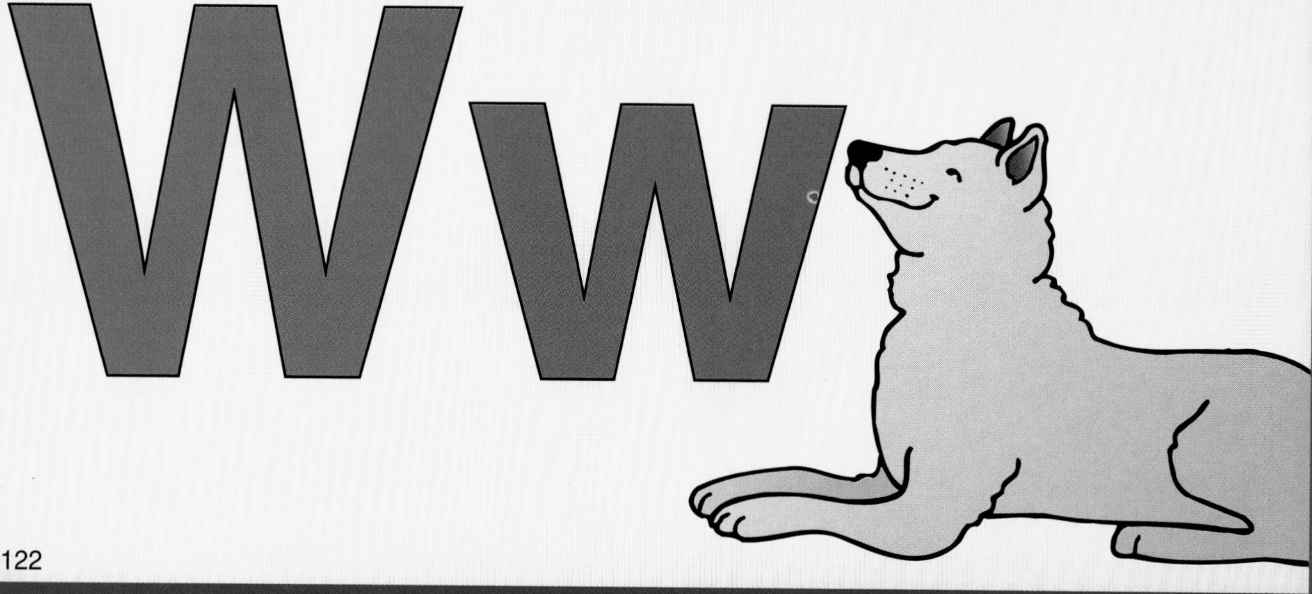

Making and Using a Wolf Headband

1. Color and cut out the headband and ears.
2. Glue the headband to the center of a 3" x 24" strip of bulletin board paper or a sentence strip.
3. Fit the strip to your head; then staple the ends together.
4. Staple or tape the ears to the sides of the headband.
5. Find someone with whom to discuss the /w/ sound.

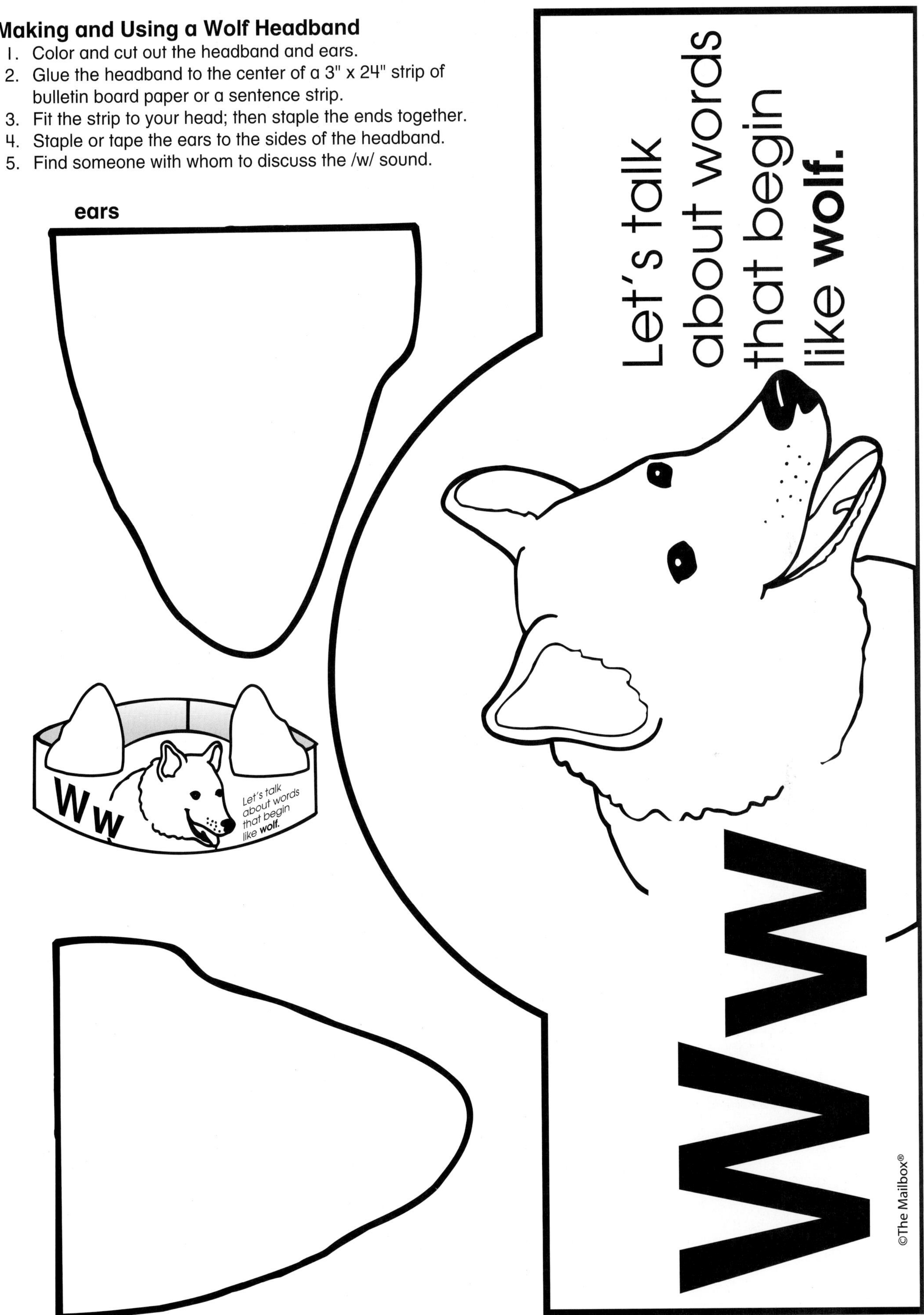

Using These Cards With "Begins Like Wolf" on Page 125

1. Before using pages 124 and 125, photocopy pages 123 and 126 for later use.
2. If desired, laminate the center mat (page 125) and the cards.
3. Cut out the cards.
4. To use, have each child place each picture whose name begins with the /w/ sound on the center mat.
5. Have the child name the pictures on the center mat, listening to confirm that they all begin like *wolf*.

Begins Like Wolf

Name____ /w/ sound

Begins Like Wolf

 Cut.

Glue.

The Beginning of X-Ray Fish

The X-Ray Fish Song

X can make a few different sounds. But in X-ray fish, it simply says its letter name. Begin your conversations about *x* with children by starting with this simple song.

(sung to the tune of "Go in and out the Window")

Say "X-ray fish," and listen.
Say "X-ray fish," and listen.
Say "X-ray fish," and listen.
X-ray begins with *x.*

Endings Instead

Since children often encounter *x* at the end of words, emphasize the /ks/ sound of *x* as an ending sound. Explain to children that although you've been talking about beginning sounds, the /ks/ sound comes often at the end of words. It's the sound that air makes as you open a can or capped bottle. Place a green square on the floor three or four feet to the left of a red square. Choose a word from the list. Starting on the green square, slowly enunciate the word as you move to the red square. Ask children whether they heard /ks/ at the beginning (when you were on the green square) or at the end (when you were on the red square). Repeat this with several words to help children get in the habit of listening for the /ks/ sound of *x* at the ends of words.

ox	jukebox
fox	mailbox
box	sandbox
chicken pox	shoebox
hatbox	toolbox

Sounds Like The Beginning of Yak

Yakkity Yak

Young learners will yearn to sing again and again when you introduce this easy song about the /y/ sound! Use a copy of the miniposter on page 16 to show your children what a yak looks like.

(sung to the tune of "Bingo")

There is a beast that starts with /y/,
And do you know its name-o?
/Y/, /y/, /y/, /y/, yak.
/Y/, /y/, /y/, /y/, yak.
/Y/, /y/, /y/, /y/, yak.
Yes! Yak is its name-o.

Yak Says Yes

Will your youngsters enjoy this circle activity? Yes, as sure as a yak has long hair! To prepare, gather a ball of yarn, a yo-yo, a whole raw yam, a square of yellow paper, and one object whose name doesn't start with the /y/ sound. Place the items inside a large yellow gift bag. If children are making the /y/ bracelet on page 129, this is a great time to have them wear the bracelets.

To play, have children sit in a circle. Hand the bag to a child and ask him to remove an item from the bag. Next, prompt the group to say, "Little yak, little yak, does it begin like *yak?"* If it does, have the child respond by saying, "Yes! *Yak* and [y word] begin the same. If the item's name does not begin with /y/, have the child silently return the item to the bag. Then have him pass the bag to the next child in the circle. Repeat the process until everyone has had a turn.

Making and Using the X-Ray Fish and Yak Bracelets

1. Color and cut out each bracelet pattern.
2. Staple the ends of the bracelet together and slip the bracelet on. Repeat wth the other bracelet.
3. Find someone with whom to discuss the letters *x* and *y*.

Using These Cards with "Begins Like X-Ray Fish" and "Begins Like Yak" on Page 131

1. Before using pages 130 and 131, photocopy pages 129 and 132 for later use.
2. If desired, laminate the center mat (page 131) and the cards.
3. Cut out the cards.
4. To use, have a child place each picture whose name begins with *x* or the /y/ sound on the center mat.
5. Have the child name the pictures on the center mat and listen to confirm that the top ones begin like *X-ray fish* and the bottom ones start with the /y/ sound of *yak.*

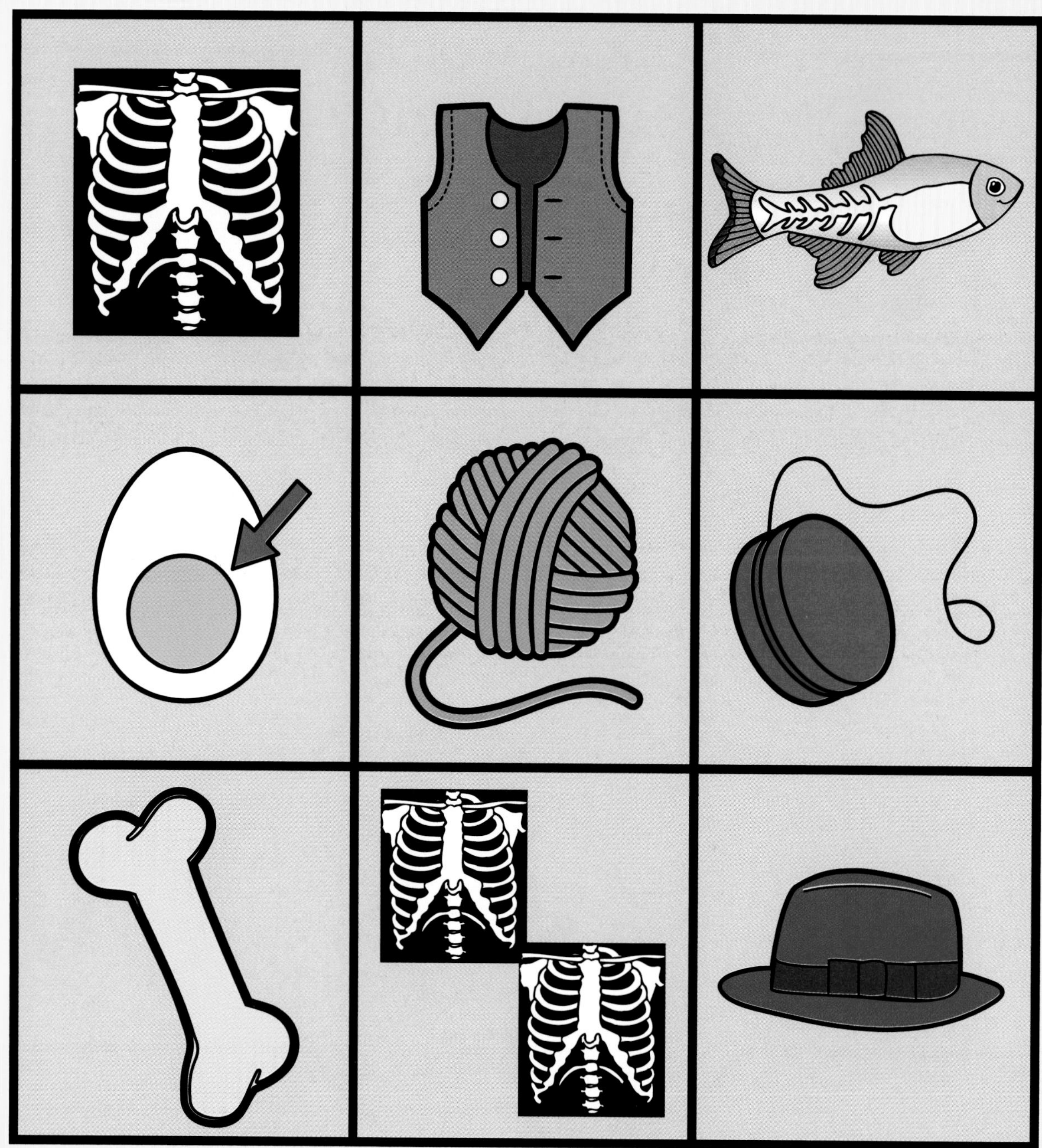

Begins Like X-Ray Fish

Name______________________________ letter name *x* and the /y/ sound

Begins Like X-Ray Fish or Yak

 Cut.

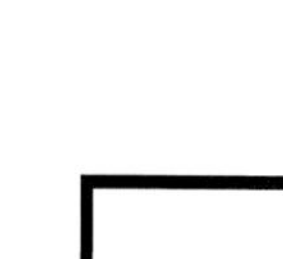 Glue.

Begins Like X-Ray Fish

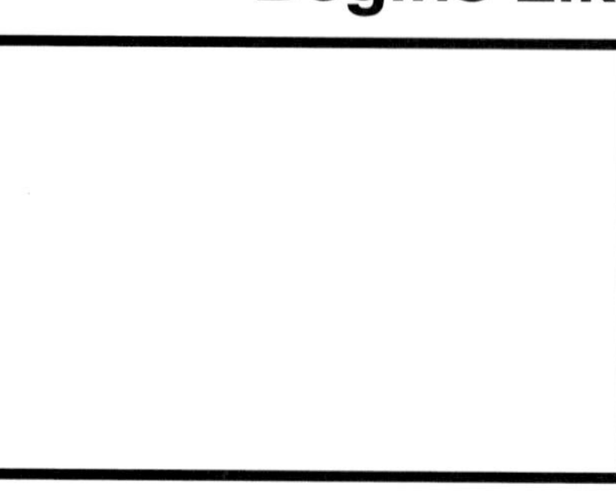

Begins Like Yak

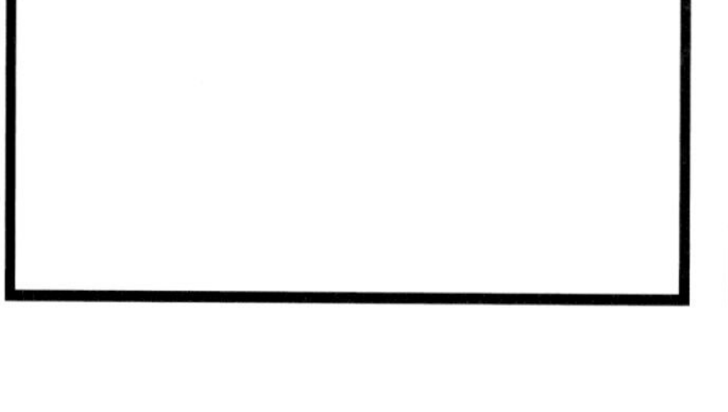

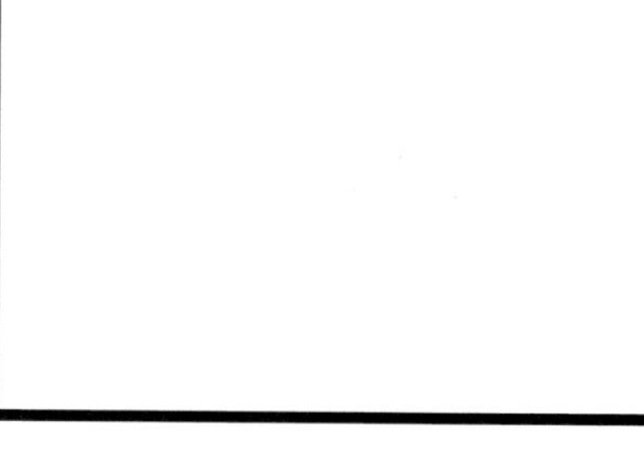

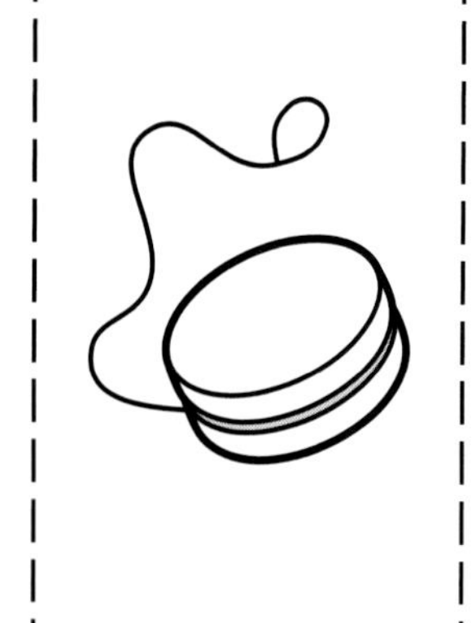

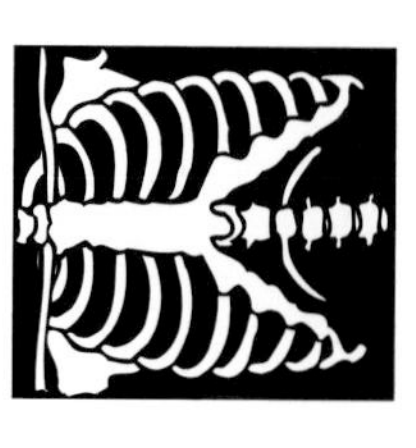

Sounds Like The Beginning of Zebra

The Zebra Song

Give your youngsters a zest for listening for the /z/ sound with this zebra song. Show a picture of a zebra and discuss the beginning sound of the word *zebra* with students. Then let the singing begin.

(sung to the tune of "Are You Sleeping?")

Zebra, zebra. Zebra, zebra.
Starts with /z/. Starts with /z/.
Come on now, let's say it.
Come on now, let's say it.
/Z/, /z/, /z/. /Z/, /z/, /z/.

Zip It!

This activity is so much fun, students will simply zip through it! To prepare, get enough zippers from your local thrift or discount store for a small group. Then gather the picture cards from page 136. To begin, give each child in a small group a zipper and invite her to sit at a table. Say the words *zebra* and *zipper* so that children can hear that they both begin with the /z/ sound. Then help each child unzip her zipper and lay it on the table. Hold up a picture card. Ask students to zip up their zippers if they hear /z/ at the beginning of the word. Then have each child unzip her zipper to be ready for the next picture card. Now that's a zippy *z!*

Zz

Z-Z-Zebra!

Get students zipping with this variation of the game Duck, Duck, Goose. Ask students to sit in a circle. Select one child to be the zebra. As the child walks around the outside of the circle, direct him to say the /z/ sound instead of the word *duck* as he taps classmates' heads. Have the child say the word *zebra* when he taps the head of the child who will stand up and chase him around the circle.

Zany Zebra Action Poem

This zesty action poem will give your youngsters some zip and reinforce the /z/ sound at the same time! Invite students to stand in a line on one side of the room, facing the opposite side. Recite the first two lines of the rhyme as students perform the actions in place. As you recite the third line, have children walk in a zigzag pattern to the opposite side of the room. On the fourth line, have them turn around and trot briskly back to the original side of the room. Finally, have students perform the fifth line's action in place. Be sure to discuss the /z/ words they hear.

I'm a zany zebra in the zoo.	*Point to self and nod head.*
Here are three things that I can do.	*Hold up three fingers.*
Zigzag back and forth.	*Walk in a zigzag pattern across the room.*
Then zip with zest!	*Trot briskly back across the room.*
But zooming is the action I like best!	*Run briskly in place.*

Making and Using a Zebra Necklace

1. Cut out both the pendant and the picture strip along the bold outer lines.
2. Staple the ends of a ¾" x 26" crepe paper streamer strip to make a necklace.
3. Fold the pendant in half, slip the streamer strip inside, and glue the folded paper closed.
4. Name the pictures on the strip, listening for the /z/ sound at the beginning of each word. Glue the picture strip to the back of the pendant.
5. Find someone with whom to discuss the /z/ sound.

/z/ picture strip

Glue the picture strip here.

Z z

Using These Cards With "Begins Like Zebra" on Page 137

1. Before using pages 136 and 137, photocopy pages 135 and 138 for later use.
2. If desired, laminate the center mat (page 137) and the cards.
3. Cut out the cards.
4. To use, have a child place each picture whose name begins with /z/ on the center mat.
5. Have the child name the pictures on the center mat, listening to confirm that they all begin like *zebra*.

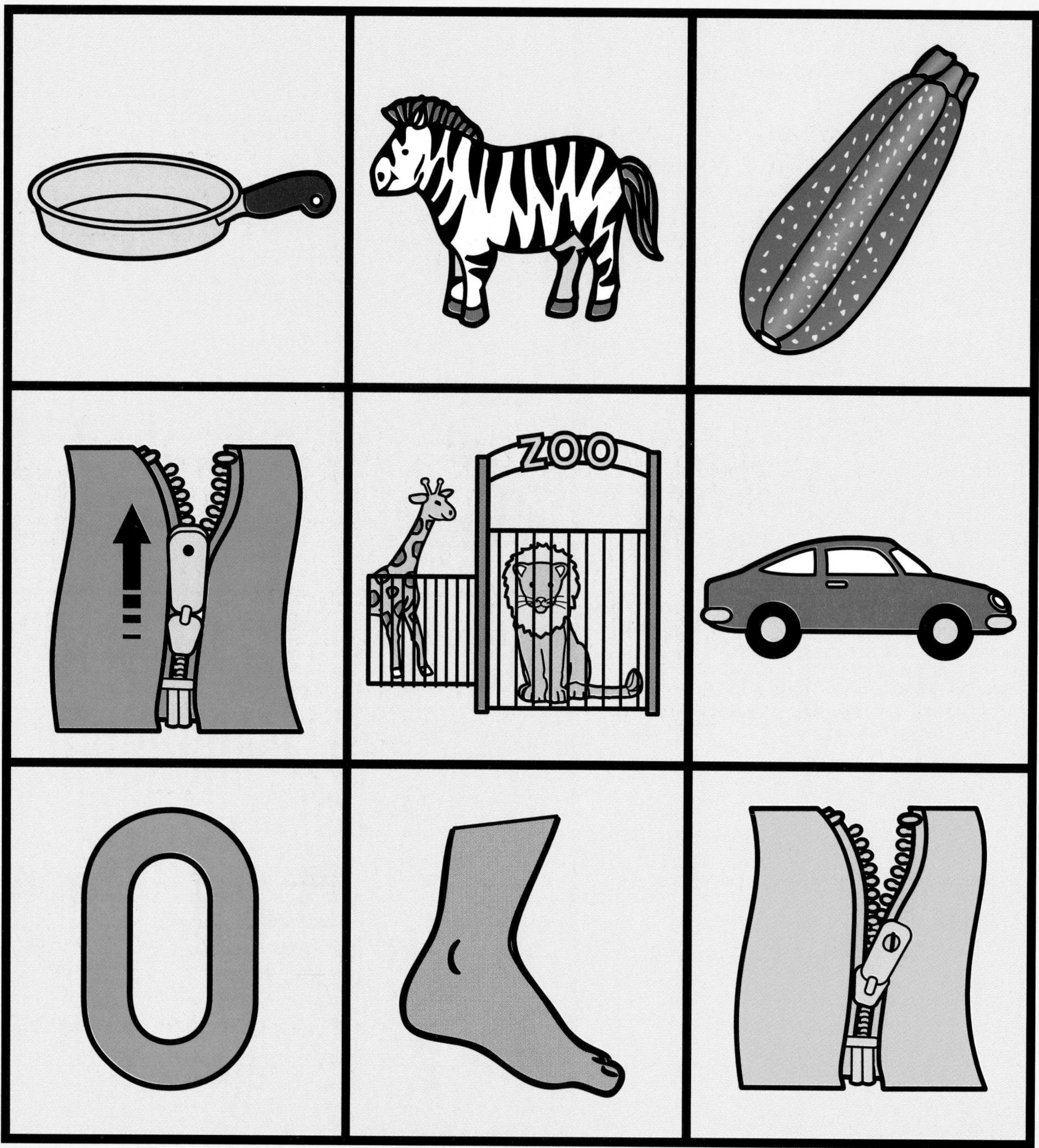

These cards may also be used with "Zip It!" on page 133.

Begins Like Zebra

Name____ /z/ sound

Begins Like Zebra

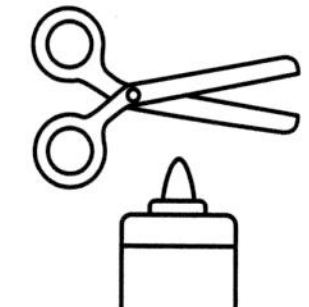
Cut.

Glue.

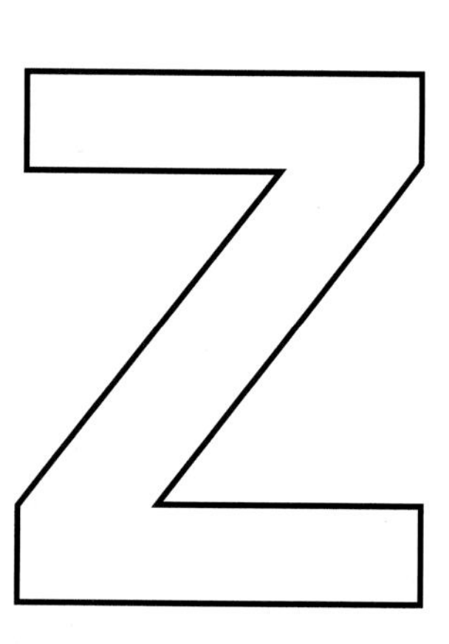

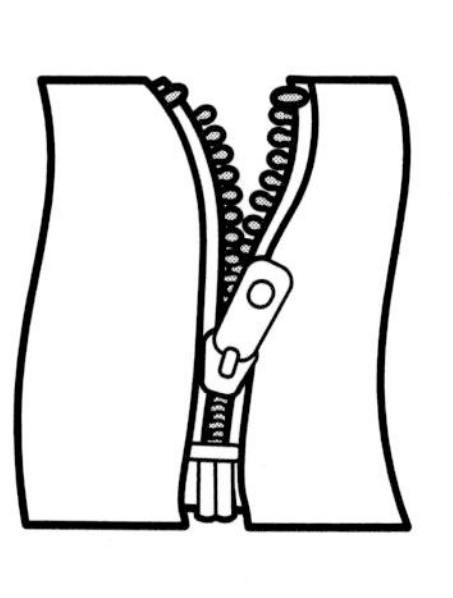
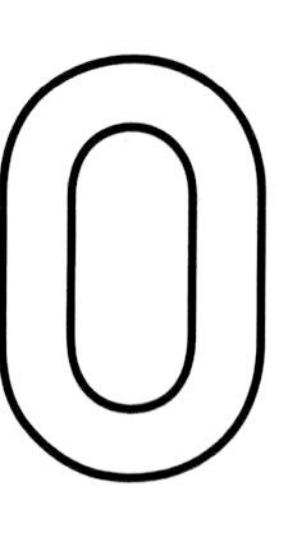

Sounds Like The Beginning of Antelope

Antelope Song

Advance your students' understanding of the short *a* sound with this song. To introduce it, display the antelope miniposter from page 8 and discuss with your students what an antelope is. Then exaggerate the beginning sound and talk about the short *a* sound. After singing the song, have children suggest other short *a* words for additional verses.

(sung to the tune of "Short'nin' Bread")

Antelope begins with /ă/. Let's say it.
Antelope begins with /ă/, /ă/, /ă/.
/Ă/; it's a good sound. Say it with me.
/Ă/; it's a good sound. Yes sirree!

Absolutely Adorable Names

Reinforce the short *a* sound by challenging children to name an antelope. To prepare, make a tagboard copy of the antelope illustration from the center mat on page 143. Cut out the antelope and glue it to a large craft stick to make a stick puppet. To begin, ask your little ones to sit in a circle. Show them the antelope stick puppet and explain that you want to give it a name that begins with the same sound as *antelope.* Then use the name list to help your youngsters brainstorm names that begin like *antelope.* As the puppet is passed from child to child, prompt them to make the short *a* sound and suggest a name that begins like *antelope.*

Abby	Andrew
Alan	Alex
Amanda	Allison
Adam	Andy
Albert	Alexander
Amber	Alyssa
Addy	Ashley
Alice	

Aa

Aerobic Antics

Here's an activity that will give students exercise and reinforce the short *a* sound at the same time. Invite children to wear their headbands (page 141) and form a circle in a large open area. Then have the children describe how antelopes move. Discuss what the word *trot* means and let the children practice trotting. Then remind them of the beginning sound of *antelope*. Explain that every time they hear a word that begins like *antelope,* they are to trot around. But if they hear a word that begins with another sound, they are to freeze in place. Call out a series of mostly short *a* words for children to respond to. After a while, discuss the word *gallop* and have youngsters practice galloping. Then repeat the activity, with children galloping around like antelopes in response to short *a* words. Whew! Who knew phonemic awareness was aerobic?

Act Like an Animal

This animal action poem is absolute fun for little ones! Use a photo-illustrated book to discuss several short *a* animals: antelope, albatross, anteater, anaconda, ant, and alligator. As you talk with your children about each animal, also talk about how each animal might move. Then lead children in saying and acting out the verse below. Afterward, say all the animal names again to see whether your children agree that they all begin the same way.

Act like an antelope with antlers on your head.	*Extend index fingers above head to look like antlers.*
Act like an albatross with your wide wings spread.	*Stretch arms out to sides; flap arms.*
Act like an anteater eating ants, not cake.	*Dart tongue out of mouth and look around.*
Act like an anaconda, a really giant snake.	*Press arms down against sides and wiggle like a snake.*
Act like a tiny ant that crawls across a dish.	*Pretend to crawl.*
Act like an alligator with an appetite for fish.	*Pretend to swim and snap jaws.*

Making and Using an Antelope Headband

1. Color and cut out the headband and horns.
2. Glue the headband to the center of a 3" x 24" strip of bulletin board paper or a sentence strip.
3. Fit the strip to your head; then staple the ends together.
4. Staple or tape the horns to the sides of the headband.
5. Find someone with whom to discuss the short *a* sound.

Using These Cards With "Begins Like Antelope" on Page 143

1. Before using pages 142 and 143, photocopy pages 141 and 144 for later use.
2. If desired, laminate the center mat (page 143) and the cards.
3. Cut out the cards.
4. To use, have a child place each picture whose name begins with the short *a* sound on the center mat.
5. Have the child name the pictures on the center mat, listening to confirm that they all begin like *antelope.*

Begins Like Antelope

Name________________________________ Short *a* sound

Begins Like Antelope

Cut.

Glue.

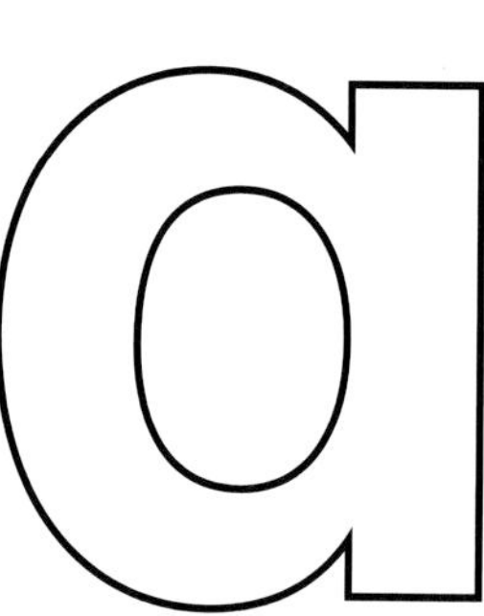

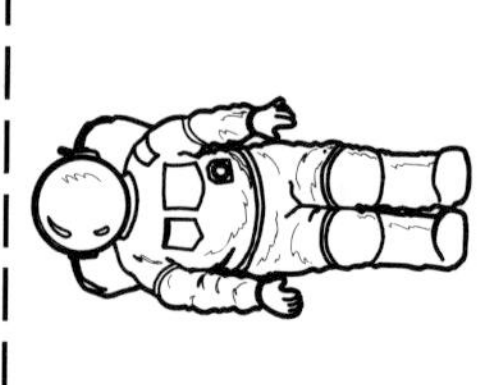

Sounds Like The Beginning of Elephant

Elephant Song

This excellent elephant tune is a nice follow-up to an introduction of the short *e* sound. Start by talking to youngsters about the sound they hear at the beginning of *elephant.* Then sing the song to allow for focusing on short *e.* Later suggest that children think of other short *e* words. Sing the song some more, replacing *elephant* with a few other /ĕ/ words for additional practice.

(sung to the tune of "Camptown Races")

Elephant begins with /ĕ/.
Listen. Listen.
Elephant begins with /ĕ/.
Say it now with me.

/Ĕ/, /ĕ/! Say it loud.
/Ĕ/, /ĕ/! Say it strong.
Elephant begins with /ĕ/.
Let's sing it all day long!

Like *Elephant* and *Egg*

Create some short *e* "egg-citement" with nine jumbo plastic eggs and the cards on page 148. Place each card in an egg. To begin the activity, remind children of the beginning sound of *elephant.* Then have them listen for the beginning sound of *egg* and decide whether *elephant* and *egg* begin alike. Ask a volunteer to crack open an egg and then decide whether the name of the picture inside begins like *egg.* Place the /ĕ/ cards in one stack and the other cards in a different stack. Have children take turns opening the remaining eggs and listening for the short *e* beginning. When all the eggs are open, read the short *e* cards as children listen to the matching beginning sounds.

Elephant Exercise

Invite students to pretend to be elephants as they chant and listen for the short *e* sound.

/Ĕ/, /ĕ/, exercise: Elephant, bend down low.	*Bend and touch hands to knees.*
/Ĕ/, /ĕ/, exercise: Elephant, touch your toes.	*Bend and touch toes.*
/Ĕ/, /ĕ/, exercise: Elephant, stretch up high.	*Stretch up on tiptoe with arms at sides.*
/Ĕ/, /ĕ/, exercise: Elephant, touch the sky.	*Stretch up on tiptoe with arms over head.*
/Ĕ/, /ĕ/, exercise: Elephant, swing your trunk.	*Slowly turn head side to side.*
/Ĕ/, /ĕ/, exercise: Elephant, swing with spunk.	*Quickly turn head and torso side to side.*
/Ĕ/, /ĕ/, exercise: Elephant, do your best.	*Jog in place and pant as if tired.*
/Ĕ/, /ĕ/, exercise: Elephant, it's time to rest!	*Sit down on the ground.*

Listening and Lumbering

Lumbering like a herd of elephants, your children will learn, listen, and laugh during this version of Musical Chairs. Place two rows of chairs back-to-back so that you have as many chairs as children. Tape a picture card to the back of each chair. You'll want most pictures to represent words with short *e* beginnings, but include a few that begin with consonants as well. To play the game, talk about the beginning sound of *elephant;* then start a recording of "Baby Elephant Walk" or any other suitably paced music. As the music plays, have children plod around the chairs like elephants, gently swinging their arms as elephant trunks. After a while, stop the music as the cue for youngsters to stop and sit. Have each child stand, in turn; name the picture on his seat; and say whether he thinks it begins like *elephant* or not. If his word is a short *e* word, he may even want to trumpet a celebratory blast through his imitation trunk! Then start the music and marching again.

Making and Using a Elephant Necklace

1. Color the elephant and its trunk.
2. Cut out the pendant, elephant's trunk, and picture strip along the bold outer lines. Glue the trunk to the pendant as indicated.
3. Staple the ends of a ¾" x 26" crepe paper streamer strip to make a necklace.
4. Fold the pendant in half, slip the streamer strip inside, and glue the folded paper closed.
5. Name the pictures on the picture strip, listening for the short *e* sound at the beginning of each word. Glue the picture strip to the back of the pendant.
6. Find someone with whom to discuss the short *e* sound.

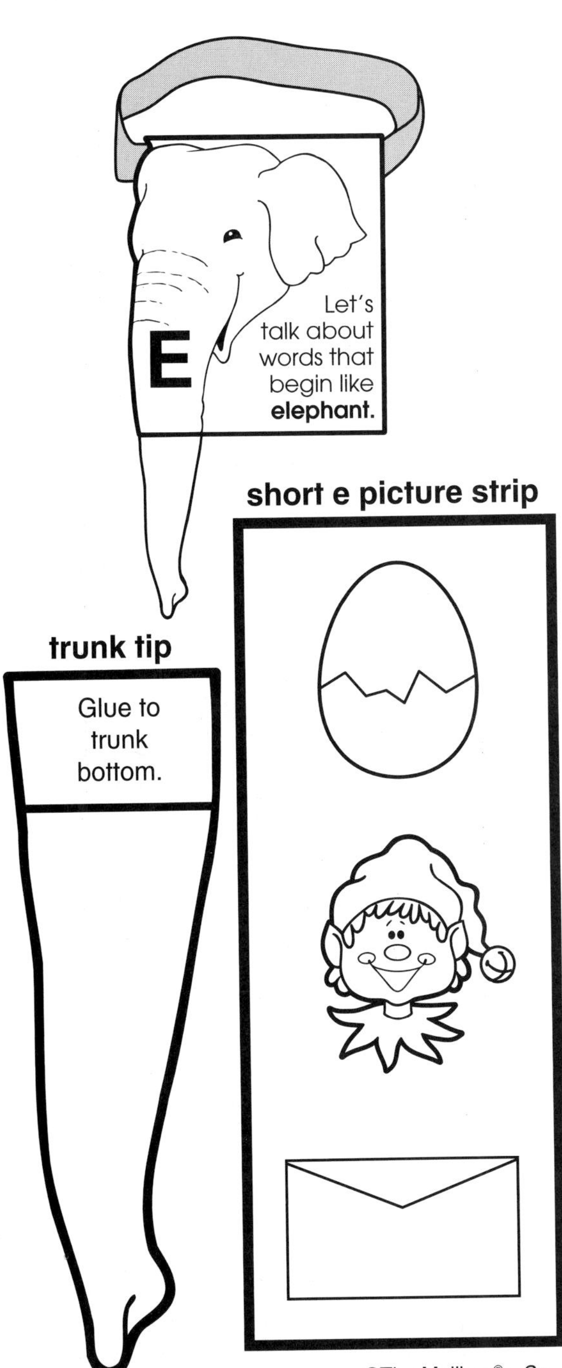

E
Let's talk about words that begin like **elephant.**

short e picture strip

trunk tip

Glue to trunk bottom.

©The Mailbox®
E
e
Glue the picture strip here.
E
Let's talk about words that begin like **elephant.**

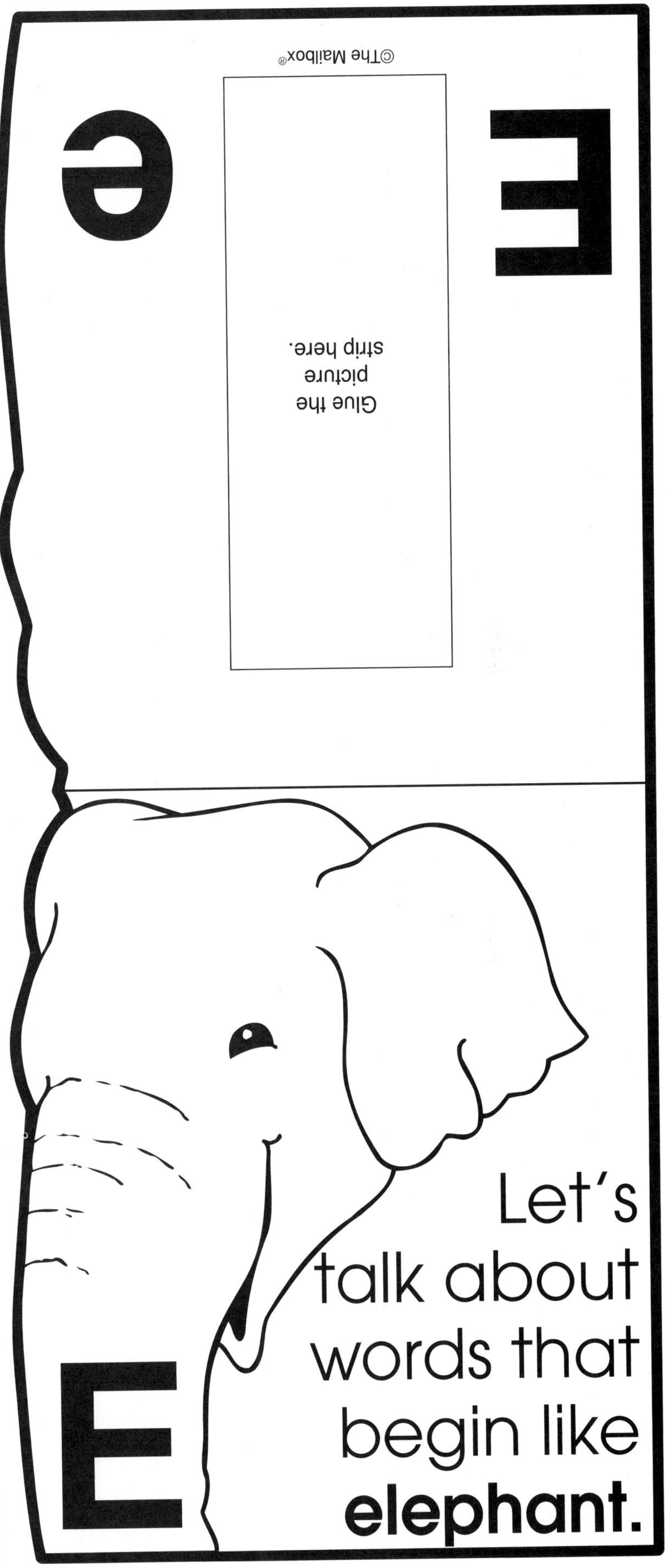

Using These Cards With "Begins Like Elephant" on Page 149

1. Before using pages 148 and 149, photocopy pages 147 and 150 for later use.
2. If desired, laminate the center mat (page 149) and the cards.
3. Cut out the cards.
4. To use, have a child place each picture whose name begins with the short *e* sound on the center mat.
5. Have the child name the pictures on the center mat, listening to confirm that they all begin like *elephant.*

These cards may also be used with "Like *Elephant* and *Egg*" on page 145.

Begins Like Elephant

Name ______________________________ Short *e* sound

Begins Like Elephant

Cut.

Glue.

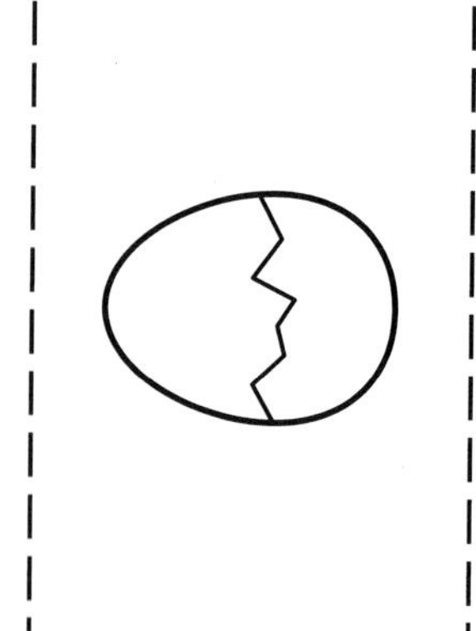

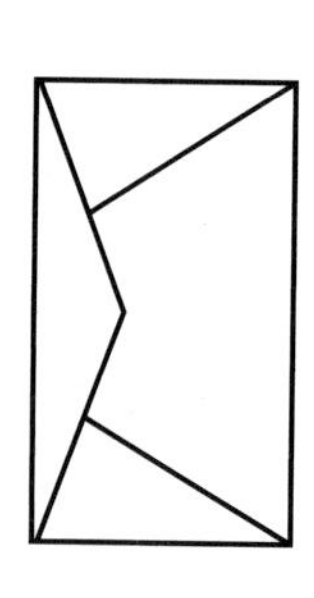

Sounds Like The Beginning of Iguana

The Iguana Song

Listening for short *i* words is cause for celebration when an iguana is your host. For extra oomph, this song includes clapping that can be replaced by having children tap out pairs of beats on triangles, rhythm sticks, or tambourines. Gather the cards from page 154. Then display an iguana picture and introduce your children to this interesting reptile. After talking about the lizard's appearance, discuss the beginning sound in *iguana.* Teach the song to your children, including either clapping or rhythm instruments, as they are seated in a circle. As children sing, put a card behind each of several children. When the verse ends, have the children who received cards name the pictures and tell the group whether or not they begin like *iguana.* Collect the cards and repeat the process again for more short *i* fun.

(sung to the tune of "If You're Happy and You Know It")

Iguana is a lizard quite well fed. *Clap, clap.*
And he has some spiny things up near his head. *Clap, clap.*
When you say a short *i* word,
He sits still and he observes.
'Cause Iguana loves the /ĭ/ words, it is said. *Clap, clap.*

Scurry, Hurry

In this short *i* game, your children scurry from place to place just like real iguanas. To prepare, scatter carpet squares on the floor in an open classroom area. To play, have children pretend to be iguanas and saunter around the squares, which are iguana hideouts. As children roam, randomly call out words—just a few of which begin with short *i.* Have children meander around until they hear a word that begins like *iguana*. Lickety-split, have them scamper quickly to put a foot on a carpet square. Then resume as before. You have to listen carefully to be one of the first iguanas back at the hideout!

Intersperse some of these words with short *i* beginnings in your word list.

if	ill
is	imagine
it	in
inch	igloo
icky	

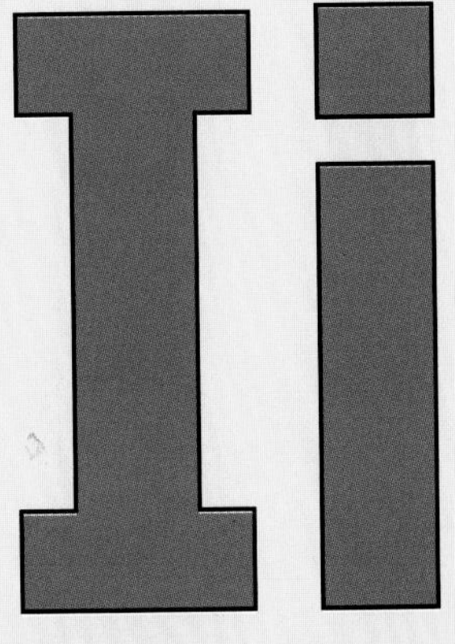

Itsy-Bitsy Iguanas

Do you hear that tapping sound? An iguana is hatching! Brainstorm with your youngsters some names for iguanas that start with the short *i* sound. Then have the group repeatedly say the chant below as each youngster, in turn, suggests a short *i* name to complete it.

Who will it be
Inside the egg?
Can't wait to see!

Tap, tap, dig, dig,
Out pops [short *i* name].
And that is that!

Isabel
Imogene
Ingrid
Ivana
Isidore
Ichabod
Iggy

Iguana Itches

Invite little ones to imitate iguanas as you reinforce the sound of short *i* with this action poem. After completing it a time or two, have children recall all the words that start the same way as *iguana*.

Insect number one buzzes near. — *Hold up one finger.*
It bites Iguana! — *Lightly swat neck.*
Iguana /ĭ/-itches from one insect bite. — *Scratch neck as if an insect bite is there.*

Insect number two buzzes near. — *Hold up two fingers.*
It bites Iguana! — *Lightly swat arm.*
Iguana /ĭ/-/ĭ/-itches from two insect bites. — *Scratch arm; then scratch neck.*

Insect number three buzzes near. — *Hold up three fingers.*
It bites Iguana! — *Lightly swat leg.*
Iguana /ĭ/-/ĭ/-/ĭ/-itches from three insect bites. — *Scratch arm, then neck, then leg.*

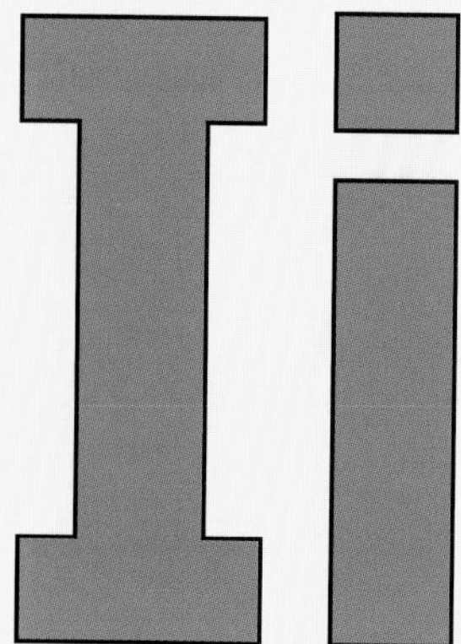

Making and Using an Iguana Bracelet

1. Color and cut out the bracelet patterns.
2. Glue the patterns back to back so the pictures show on both sides.
3. Staple the ends together and slip the bracelet on.
4. Find someone with whom to discuss the short *i* sound.

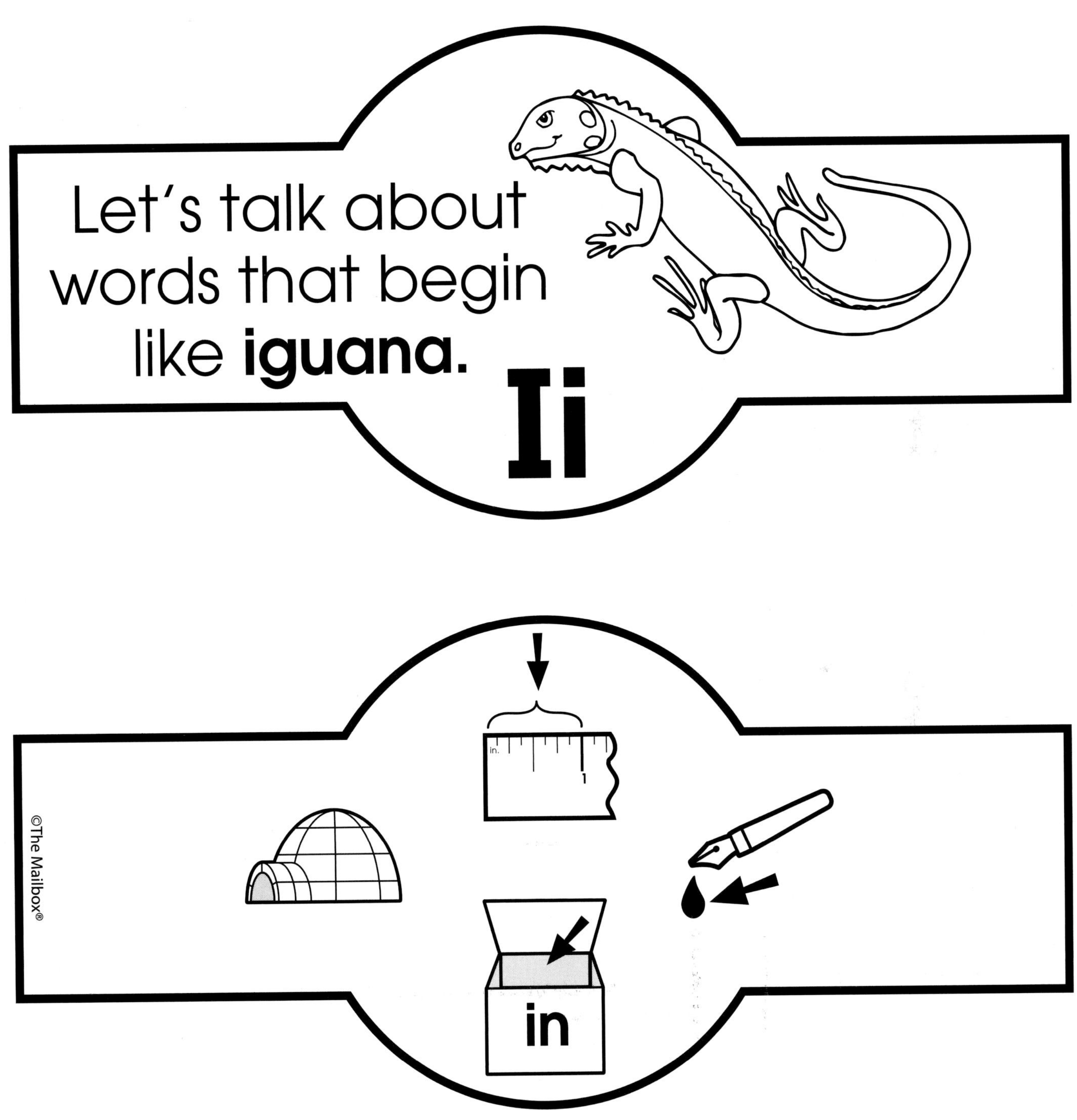

Using These Cards With "Begins Like Iguana" on Page 155

1. Before using pages 154 and 155, photocopy pages 153 and 156 for later use.
2. If desired, laminate the center mat (page 155) and the cards.
3. Cut out the cards.
4. To use, have a child place each picture whose name begins with the short *i* sound on the center mat.
5. Have the child name the pictures on the center mat, listening to confirm that they all begin like *iguana*.

These cards may also be used with "The Iguana Song" on page 151.

Begins Like Iguana

Name ____________________

Begins Like Iguana

Cut.

Glue.

Sounds Like

The Beginning of Otter

Otter Opera

Opportunities for learning abound when your little ones sing this song. Show your children a picture of an otter and discuss what they know about otters. Then talk about the word *otter* and its beginning sound. Teach children the song below. When children know it well, have them suggest other short *o* words for additional versions.

(sung to the tune of "Are You Sleeping?")

Otter, otter. Otter, otter.
Starts with /ŏ/. Starts with /ŏ/.
Come on now, let's say it.
Come on now, let's say it.
/Ŏ/, /ŏ/, /ŏ/. /Ŏ/, /ŏ/, /ŏ/.

Otter's Objects

Reinforce the short *o* sound with this small-group activity. Gather the picture cards from page 160. Place a large paper *o* cutout on a table with a picture of an otter and invite a small group of youngsters to join you there. Hold up each card, in turn, and say its name. If students hear /ŏ/ at the beginning of the word, put the card on the letter *o*. Follow up by asking children to think of other words that begin like *otter.*

Where Is That Rascally Otter?

In this seek-and-find game, youngsters go scampering off in search of otters and come scampering back ready to listen for short *o* words. Trim off the lower half of the pendant pattern on page 159 and make a class supply. Cut out the copies and place them around the room just before this game begins. To play, divide your class into two teams. Have the first player retrieve an otter cutout, listen as you say three words (see the list shown, reading straight across), and tell you which one starts like *otter.* If he is correct, have him pat his tummy otter-style (once for locating the otter and once for identifying the short *o* word). Continue the game in this way, alternating teams until the otters have been found. When the game comes to an end, great phonemic awareness is one "otter-ific" result!

Word List for Game

fish	odd	clam
splash	water	opposite
fur	slide	officer
weasel	dive	ox
paws	operate	river
October	claws	icy
squeal	pups	opera
octagon	growl	swim
capture	appetite	option
chirp	oxygen	tail
osprey	whiskers	tummy
burrow	bank	octopus
olive	snail	insect
catch	ostrich	wet

Rolling Around

In this game, short *o* pictures roll around as otters sometimes do. To prepare, make two copies of the picture cards from page 160 and cover two cubical boxes with Con-Tact covering. Tape six of the pictures from one page to the sides of a box, including at least one picture that doesn't start with the short *o* sound. Do the same with the second box, using the other page of pictures. To play, have a child roll both cubes and determine how many of the upturned pictures start like *otter.* Give him a point for each short *o* word correctly identified. Continue in this way with children taking turns rolling the boxes and determining the number of picture names that begin with the short *o* sound. End the activity by complimenting children on their terrific ability to distinguish sounds.

Oo

Making and Using an Otter Necklace

1. Color the otter.
2. Cut out the pendant and the picture strip along the bold outer lines.
3. Staple the ends of a ¾" x 26" crepe paper streamer strip to make a necklace.
4. Fold the pendant in half, slip the streamer strip inside, and glue the folded paper closed.
5. Name the pictures on the picture strip, listening for the short *o* sound at the beginning of each word. Glue the picture strip to the back of the pendant.
6. Find someone with whom to discuss the short *o* sound.

Let's talk about words that begin like **otter.**
Oo

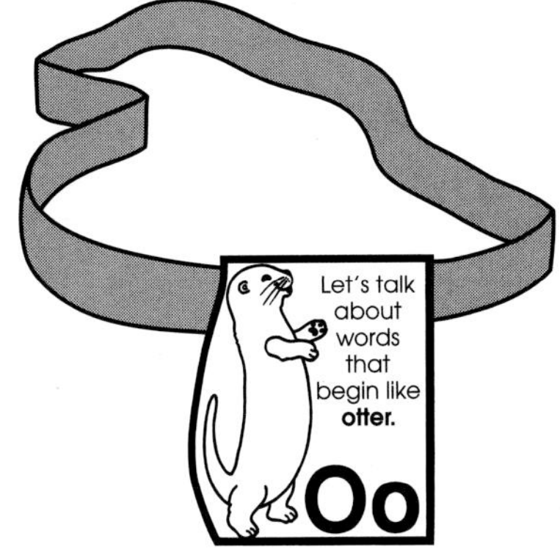

short *o* picture strip

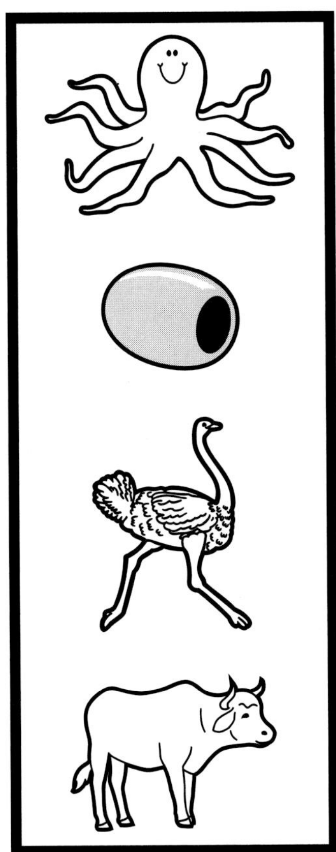

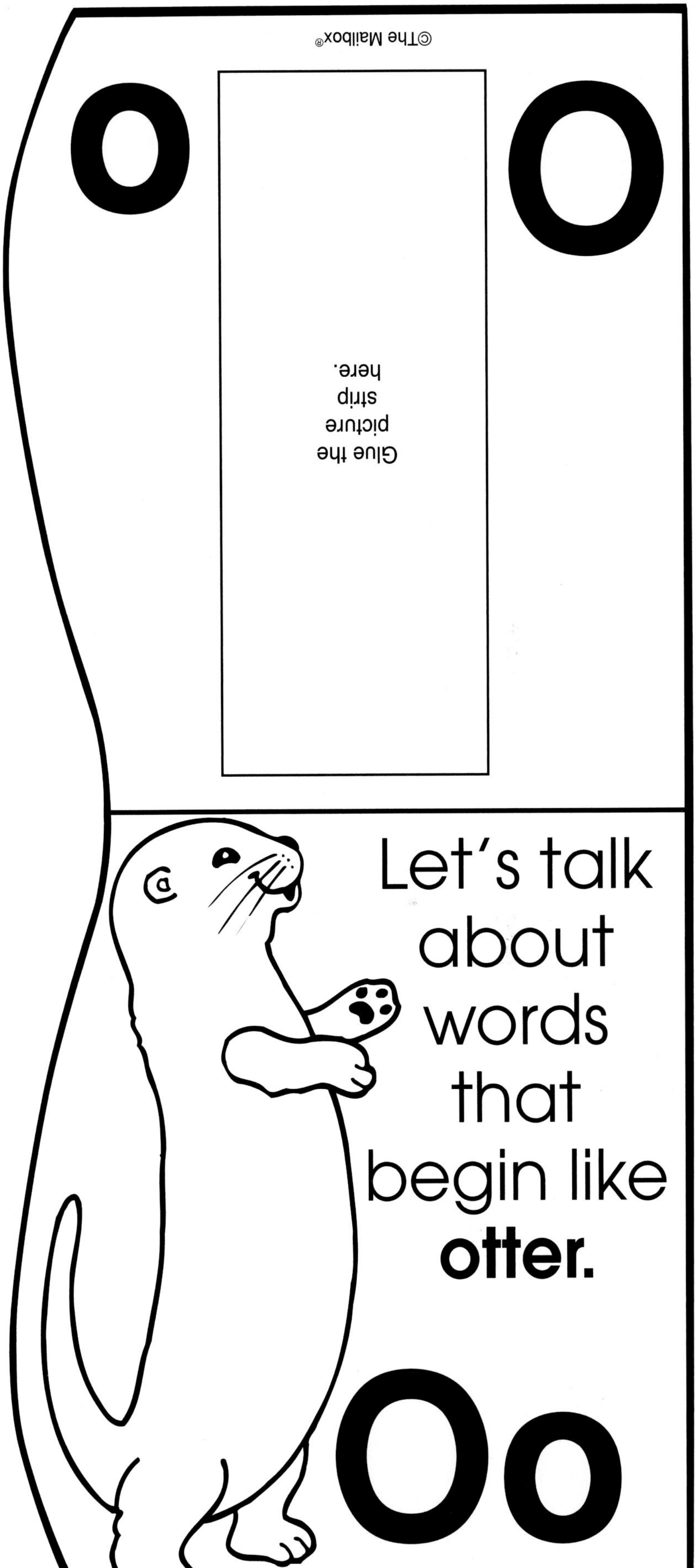

©The Mailbox®
o
O
Glue the picture strip here.
Let's talk about words that begin like **otter.**
Oo

Using These Cards With "Begins Like Otter" on Page 161

1. Before using pages 160 and 161, photocopy pages 159 and 162 for later use.
2. If desired, laminate the center mat (page 161) and the cards.
3. Cut out the cards.
4. To use, have a child place each picture whose name begins with the short *o* sound on the center mat.
5. Have the child name the pictures on the center mat, listening to confirm that they all begin like *otter.*

These cards may also be used with "Otter's Objects" on page 157 and "Rolling Around" on page 158.

Begins Like Otter

Name ______________________________ short *o* sound

Begins Like Otter

Cut.

Glue.

Sounds Like The Beginning of Umbrella Cockatoo

The Umbrella Cockatoo Song

Listening for the sound of short *u* is a lot of fun with this umbrella cockatoo tune. Show children a picture of an umbrella cockatoo and talk about the bird and its beginning sound. Then launch into this tune to make the discussion really memorable.

(sung to the tune of "The Farmer in the Dell")

Umbrella cockatoo,
Umbrella cockatoo,
Um-brel-la starts with /ŭ/.
Umbrella cockatoo.

Umbrella cockatoo,
Umbrella cockatoo,
Um-brel-la, /ŭ/, /ŭ/, /ŭ/.
Umbrella cockatoo.

Over by the Umbrellas

When you start setting up umbrellas for this short *u* game, children will start checking the sky for ominous clouds. Good news—no rain is required! Place several open umbrellas handle to handle to form a ring of colorful canopies. Play a rhythmic musical recording softly in the background. As children walk in random paths around the umbrellas, call out words that do not begin with the short *u* sound. Occasionally, include a word that begins with /ŭ/. When the children hear a short *u* word, have them touch the nearest umbrella and freeze. Talk about the word's /ŭ/ sound, comparing it to the beginning sound of *umbrella*. Then begin the process again. Umbrellas, music, and words certainly do make phonemes fun!

Up and Under, Umbrella Cockatoo!

Phonemic awareness and the use of directional words will take flight with this bird-themed idea. To prepare, make a tagboard copy of the umbrella cockatoo illustration from the center mat on page 167. Cut it out and glue it to a large craft stick to make a stick puppet. Then set up an obstacle course with several small chairs so that the umbrella cockatoo stick puppet can be moved up on the tops of the chairs and then under them.

To play, invite students to form a circle around the course. Show them the puppet and explain that its name, *umbrella cockatoo,* comes from the fancy feathers on the bird's head! Mention that the words *up, under,* and *umbrella* all start with the same beginning sound, the short *u* sound. Next, tell students that they are going to help an umbrella cockatoo move through the obstacle course. Ask each child, in turn, to give the umbrella cockatoo instructions that include *up* or *under* as you (or a child) move the puppet to approach a chair. Prompt the child to give his directions in a complete sentence followed by "Up, umbrella cockatoo, up!" or "Under, umbrella cockatoo, under!" as a trainer might coax. Then move the puppet to the position indicated by the child.

Umbrellas Up!

Reinforce your youngsters' understanding of the /ŭ/ sound with this small-group activity. To prepare, purchase enough paper party drink umbrellas from your local discount store for a small group if desired. (Otherwise, plan to have children act out the opening of umbrellas instead.) Then gather the picture cards from page 166.

To begin, give each child in a small group an umbrella. Or demonstrate for children how they can pretend their bodies are umbrellas—lifting their arms opens the umbrella. Either way, show students how to carefully open and close their umbrellas. Hold up a picture card and name it. Ask students to put their umbrellas up if they hear /ŭ/ at the beginning of the word. Talk about the students' responses. Then have each child close her umbrella to be ready for the next picture card. Continue in this manner, using all your cards and perhaps some oral words too.

Making and Using an Umbrella Cockatoo Necklace

1. Color around the umbrella cockatoo, leaving its feathers white.
2. Cut out the pendant and the picture strip along the bold outer lines.
3. Staple the ends of a ¾" x 26" crepe paper streamer strip to make a necklace.
4. Fold the pendant in half, slip the streamer strip inside, and glue the folded paper closed.
5. Name the pictures on the picture strip, listening for the short *u* sound at the beginning of each word. Glue the picture strip to the back of the pendant.
6. Find someone with whom to discuss the short *u* sound.

short *u* picture strip

Using These Cards With "Begins Like Umbrella Cockatoo" on Page 167

1. Before using pages 166 and 167, photocopy pages 165 and 168 for later use.
2. If desired, laminate the center mat (page 167) and the cards.
3. Cut out the cards.
4. To use, have a child place each picture whose name begins with the short *u* sound on the center mat.
5. Have the child name the pictures on the center mat, listening to confirm that they all begin like *umbrella cockatoo.*

These cards may also be used with "Umbrellas Up!" on page 164.

Begins Like
Umbrella
Cockatoo

Name ____________________ Short *u* sound

Begins Like Umbrella Cockatoo

Cut.

Glue.

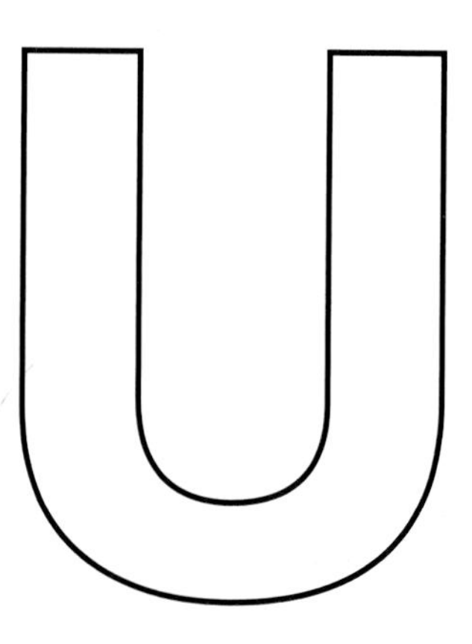